D1499766

A MAN &
HIS CAR

ALSO BY MATT HRANEK

A Man & His Watch

A MAN & HIS CAR

ICONIC CARS AND STORIES
FROM THE MEN WHO LOVE THEM

MATT HRANEK

ARTISAN | NEW YORK

Library of Congress Cataloging-in-Publication Data

Names: Hranek, Matt, author.
Title: A man & his car / Matt Hranek.
Other titles: A man and his car
Description: New York : Artisan, a division of Workman Publishing Co., Inc., 2020. | Includes index.
Identifiers: LCCN 2020003888 | ISBN 9781579658922
Subjects: LCSH: Automobiles—Anecdotes.
Classification: LCC GV1023 .H73 2020 | DDC 629.222—dc23
LC record available at https://lccn.loc.gov/2020003888

Design by Nina Simoneaux

Photographs by Matt Hranek except as noted below:

Page 10: Michael Hrizuk; page 13: Courtesy of Matt Hranek; pages 46–47: Courtesy of Afshin Behnia; page 136: Object ID: 00.136.137: From the Collections of The Henry Ford. Gift of Ford Motor Company;
page 137 (top): Object ID: 29.1009.1: From the Collections of The Henry Ford. Gift of Albert Boyer; page 137 (bottom): Object ID: 71.82.1: From the Collections of The Henry Ford. Gift of Elizabeth Burroughs Kelley;
page 138 (top): Object ID: 56.79.1: From the Collections of The Henry Ford; page 138 (bottom): Object ID: 66.47.1: From the Collections of The Henry Ford. Gift of Ford Motor Company; page 139: Object ID: 50.11.1:
From the Collections of The Henry Ford. Gift of Ford Motor Company, Lincoln-Mercury Division; page 140: Object ID: 67.74.1: From the Collections of The Henry Ford. Gift of Ford Motor Company, Lincoln-Mercury Division;
page 141 (top): Object ID: 78.4.1: From the Collections of The Henry Ford. Gift of Ford Motor Company; page 141 (bottom): Object ID: 92.104.1: From the Collections of The Henry Ford. Gift of Ford Motor Company;
page 214: Courtesy of Ted Gushue; pages 229 and 230–231: Courtesy of Kenneth Bailey; pages 232 and 235: Courtesy of Peter Harholdt; page 240: Stephen Lewis.

Artisan books are available at special discounts when purchased in bulk for premiums and sales
promotions as well as for fund-raising or educational use. Special editions or book excerpts also
can be created to specification. For details, contact the Special Sales Director at the address
below, or send an e-mail to specialmarkets@workman.com.

For speaking engagements, contact speakersbureau@workman.com.

Published by Artisan
A division of Workman Publishing Co., Inc.
225 Varick Street
New York, NY 10014-4381
artisanbooks.com

Artisan is a registered trademark of Workman Publishing Co., Inc.

Published simultaneously in Canada by Thomas Allen & Son, Limited

Printed in China

First printing, September 2020

1 3 5 7 9 10 8 6 4 2

This book is dedicated to my favorite passenger and navigator, who not only shares my passion for cars but also indulges me with my own collection: my wife, Yolanda.

CONTENTS

PHOTOGRAPHING A 1912 HUDSON SPEEDSTER
(SEE PAGE 100) AT THE HILTON HEAD
CONCOURS D'ELEGANCE

PREFACE

My love for cars starts with my father. It's fair to say he was obsessed with them. We went to car shows on the weekends, and he'd point out certain cars whenever we were driving. He loved English cars—he owned a 1959 Triumph TR3A—and also Chevy pickups. He was a professional sign painter and illustrator who gravitated to the old-school arts, and he used to letter drag racers and pinstripe antique cars. He would also be persuaded by my cousins to monogram their Camaros. We'd go to Five Mile Point Speedway, which was a dirt track, watch the cars race around, and admire all the vehicles in its parking lots.

I've always loved European sports cars, probably because of my dad. My first car was a '71 BMW I bought from my uncle Junie. I nearly drove it into the ground—and then my brother really drove it into the ground. All my cousins loved American muscle cars: Trans Ams, GTOs, Firebirds, Camaros. They would buy the cars and then soup up the engines to make them their own. When people ask me, "What's your dream car?" I tell them I already own it. It's my 1987 Porsche 911 Carrera Targa (see page 21). That was the car I had a poster of on my wall in high school. (Though, actually, that one probably had the whale tail.)

It was a real challenge to put this book together. For my previous book, *A Man & His Watch*, many of the contributors shipped their watches to me, and the photographer and I shot each one in the

"Owning a car can be a benchmark of success or a way to become the version of yourself you've always wanted to be. It can remind you of the important people in your life or bring you closer to them."

—MATT HRANEK

WITH MY 1971 BMW BAVARIA IN THE BACKYARD OF MY CHILDHOOD HOME IN BINGHAMTON, NEW YORK

studio. It was obviously more complicated to photograph cars—they are, simply, big machines. So I had a 30-by-30-foot black backdrop made, and I schlepped that thing all over the world: on trains, on airplanes, in taxicabs, in the back of my Land Rover. The owners and I didn't wash the cars, didn't alter them or refresh them. Against the black, all the detail could be seen, and we wanted to celebrate the patina, the wear—the storytelling inherent in the object. It was a real labor of love. I also photographed the cars the way designers expect them to be seen: in daylight, with front, side, and back views. That's how cars are conceived. You see them coming toward you, passing you in profile, then moving away from you.

This edit is very personal to me—there are countless car stories out there, but the ones you'll find here are about cars that I love, the types of vehicles that have shaped my own love affair with the automobile. In talking to so many men about their cars, I noticed that nobody had to think about what his meant to him or why. Every time I said, "Hey, tell me about this car. What's the significance? What's your emotional connection?" the guy would launch into the story without hesitation, as if he'd been thinking about it for a very long time. Which, of course, he surely had.

Cars do that. You create a bond with them. Owning a car can be a benchmark of success or a way to become the version of yourself you've always wanted to be. It can remind you of the important people in your life or bring you closer to them. This was never going to be a book about priceless, expensive automobiles (though there are more than a few of those in here, too). This is a book about the stories we tell about our cars—intimate, emotional, thoughtful, and sometimes funny stories about these amazing machines—and, more important, about the stories our cars tell about us.

—Matt Hranek

JAY LENO

COMEDIAN & TV HOST

1955 BUICK ROADMASTER

I was born in New York but grew up in a rural area of New England. It was an era when you could buy old cars for twenty bucks, fifty bucks—people just abandoned them. My friends and I got an old Renault 4CV running. We were twelve, just driving around the field, our moms watching us through kitchen windows. Now Child Protective Services would be called.

It was a more mechanical age. It was before Netflix, so you'd find stuff to do. People would take things apart and put them back together—watches, crystal radios. Car magazines were black-and-white. I remember those old issues of *Road & Track*, the images of Carroll Shelby standing with a Cobra, the GT40, the Mustang. Those were iconic images—cars you had to see in a magazine because you'd never see them in person. You'd hang out outside a McDonald's all night and go home at 11:00 and hear later that a Corvette came through at 11:30 and you'd think, *I missed it! I missed the Corvette!* I remember we had a Lamborghini Espada go through town when I was a kid. It was a huge deal. Now you just go on the internet, see whatever you want.

My dad wasn't a car guy. To this day, he doesn't understand why an old car would cost more than a new one. In 1966, we went to Shawsheen Motors and my dad says to the salesman, "Where are the full-size cars?" He'd just buy what was on the showroom floor. "Give me that one." The salesman says, "Mr. Leno, you can order a big car, but it will take four to six weeks." My dad's grumbling, but he orders the car. I ask if I can pick the engine, and my mother says, "Let the boy pick the engine. What difference does it make?" So I'm sixteen years old, and I know I'm going to be driving the thing. I pull the salesman aside and say: "I want the big Galaxie, 428 engine, CCX heavy-duty automatic, 370 gears. Police-pursuit package with the muffler-delete option."

Six weeks later, the car arrives at the dealer. My dad walks in and goes, "It's got bucket seats!" Then he turns the key and the car goes *RUHHMMM-RUMRUMM* and my dad says, "There's a hole in the goddamn muffler! It's a brand-new car and there's a hole in the goddamn muffler!" The salesman keeps showing him the paperwork, saying, "No, Mr. Leno, this is what you ordered, the muffler-delete option." Now my dad is ripshit. "What the hell do you mean, *police pursuit*? What did you have me buy?" He's screaming at me, screaming at the salesman. We get in the car, he starts it up,

puts it in gear, and then: "This thing, it's a goddamn rocket ship!" He didn't speak to me for a week. But a month or two later, I'm in my parents' room looking for something, and I see he got a ticket for going 110. He was the coolest guy in the insurance sales office.

I've had this Buick Roadmaster longer than any other car. Since '72. One day in the early seventies, I was sitting in my apartment in Boston, and I realized that if I stayed there any longer, I was going to want to acquire stuff, move to a better place. My friends were getting married, buying houses, things like that. I said, "I'm going to California right now," and walked out of my apartment. I told my neighbor, "Take whatever you want," and I left.

Johnny Carson had just moved to California. *The Tonight Show* was in Los Angeles. Merv Griffin was in Los Angeles. Everything was in California.

I land at LAX and say to the cabdriver, "Take me to the Sunset Strip." He goes, "How much money you got?" I say, "I got fifty bucks." He drops me way down Sunset, on Western somewhere. I walk five miles to the Comedy Store and end up sleeping on the back stairs for a week or so.

I picked up a copy of the *PennySaver* and saw a '55 Buick for 350 bucks. Don't forget, I bought that car in '72. That would be like going to LA today and buying a car from the late nineties.

Okay, it's a big car. I could sleep in it. I didn't have a place to live, but it's LA—you always get a car before you get a place to live. I slept in the car for a while, usually in the drugstore parking lot after sunset. It was fine. I had it all.

I met my wife, and we dated in this car. I parked it in my future mother-in-law's driveway in Encino. Other cars came along. Newer cars, younger cars, fancier cars. The Buick just sat there. For seventeen years.

One day I went over to my mother-in-law's house and there's a note on the windshield that says, "Somebody obviously doesn't care about this car. I'd love to buy it." I said, "I care about this car!" I felt awful.

By that time in the early nineties, I had acquired a garage. I dragged the car back here, and the guys and I did a total restoration, put a Big Block 572 in it, Corvette suspension, Corvette brakes, made our own hubcaps. Put 17-inch wheels on it to make it look a little bigger.

When I got the job guest-hosting *The Tonight Show*, I took this car to the lot. I took it to my first day at *The Tonight Show*, and I took it to my last day at *The Tonight Show*. It's a memorable car for me.

My wife and I first made out in the Buick. After twenty-five years, I said, "Let's try to find the place where we first made out." Of course, it's a housing development now. I said, "I think it's right here," and we're basically in some guy's driveway. It's two in the morning. We're not quite as agile as we used to be. I lean on the horn—*EEEEP!* Her hair's stuck—*EEEEP!* A porch light comes on. Some guy comes out, and we're in the front seat like, "Sorry, sorry!"

My wife's not crazy about that story.

"I didn't have a place to live, but it's LA—you always get a car before you get a place to live. I slept in the car for a while, usually in the drugstore parking lot after sunset. It was fine. I had it all."

—JAY LENO

MATT HRANEK

AUTHOR & PHOTOGRAPHER

———— H ————

1987 PORSCHE 911 CARRERA TARGA & JOHN DEERE GATOR

I've been a car guy all my life. My father was a big influence on that. He loved British cars, had a 1959 Triumph TR3A.

I grew up in Upstate New York, not too far from Watkins Glen. There's an amazing dirt racetrack called Five Mile Point Speedway, where we used to go as kids. They sold a bumper sticker that said, "If you don't have dirt in your beer, you haven't been to a real car race." My uncles were all gearheads, always had old Impalas around, and my cousins were into cars, buying old Firebirds and restoring them. My cousin Jimmy, in particular, had the coolest cars—brand-new, off-the-lot Firebirds, Trans Ams, Corvette Stingrays.

I was always looking at European sports cars, and particularly Porsches. I had a poster of a 911 Targa in my room. I loved everything about it—the shape, the sounds of the car.

This 911 Targa came to be mine in an extraordinary way. Yolanda, my wife, had been dating this guy in San Francisco, Ira Sandler. Yolanda's a real car person. She felt that as a big club owner, he needed to represent a bit better than his rusted-out Volkswagen Rabbit, so she takes him to a car auction. This chocolate-brown 1987 Porsche 911 Carrera Targa pulls out on the lot. She says, "You need to buy that." So he does.

Fast-forward. Yolanda and Ira haven't been dating for years but remain very close. Ira's still in San Francisco, and Yolanda and I go out to meet him. At this point, he's driving a new Audi, and the Porsche is just decaying in a garage. Yolanda and I have been planning a drive down to Palm Springs to meet friends for New Year's Eve, and she asks Ira if we can borrow the Porsche. He says, "Sure, take the car."

We end up eloping in Palm Springs on New Year's Day. It had been such a powerful, amazing, intensely romantic road trip. So epic. But I have to give the car back. As I reluctantly hand over the keys to Ira, I look at it and think, *God, someday.*

A couple of years down the road, I'm helping Ira with a house project. He asks me what I want for my efforts, and I say, "Ira, I want the Porsche." Back then, those cars weren't commanding a lot in terms of price, and it needed TLC—minor interior stuff, some mechanicals. And Ira says, "Okay, deal. You can have the car."

It meant so much to me. Yolanda found that car. We eloped in that car. People have said to me, "What's your fantasy car? If you could own any car, what would it be?" It's that Carrera. That 911 Targa with the tan interior and the CD that my friend Fred made that has all the best music of 1987, on the winding roads of Upstate New York, thinking about that eighties version of myself and how dreams can come true in such a simple and perfect way.

I will have this car until I die, and when I do, I want my daughter to go into the barn and peel back the cover and have her heart race and her eyes dilate the same way mine do. These cars become an extension of you. It's a connection.

My other favorite car is also stored in that barn. It's a six-wheeled John Deere Gator. Diesel engine. We call it the "country convertible." We got it when we first bought our farm.

I don't know what I would do without that thing. It's got a dump bed, so it's great for hauling stuff, like materials to build houses; it's terrific in the snow. But really, it's more of a car than a tractor. I taught my daughter to drive on that thing. All my neighbors drive around in their Gators, stop by or meet up for a beer in their Gators. We're up in the country—no one jumps in the car to go down the road; they jump in the Gator.

Throw a bunch of kids and dogs in the back, some towels, and you're off to the pond for a swim. It's just so fun and practical. I love it deeply.

BRUCE MEYER

FOUNDING CHAIRMAN,
PETERSEN AUTOMOTIVE MUSEUM (SEE PAGE 60)

———— || ————

1962 COBRA CSX2001 & 1965 BIZZARRINI A3/C 0222

Being a Southern California boy and a hot-rodder, I'm partial to anything with an American V8 engine. The Shelby fits the bill, as does the 1965 Bizzarrini—not only is it a Le Mans race car that won its class in 1965, but it's also powered by an American V8, a 327 Chevrolet.

The story of Giotto Bizzarrini is one of great interest to me. He was a race car savant, a race engineer savant. He graduated from technical school in Italy in 1953 and was immediately hired by Alfa Romeo, where he became renowned for his engineering skills and problem-solving. Enzo Ferrari found out about him and hired him away from Alfa four years later.

Bizzarrini was the real secret behind so much of Ferrari's race car success in the late fifties and early sixties. He designed the GTO, which is maybe Ferrari's most famous, landmark car. Then, in 1961, the company had what has been called the "Palace Revolt," when Enzo summarily fired the entire racing group, including Bizzarrini.

But Bizzarrini still had that passion for building race cars, and he eventually started his own company. He built this car and drove it to Le Mans in 1965. The car won its class, finishing in the top ten, and he drove it home. It was the second-fastest car at Le Mans that year, behind only the big-block Ford GT40, which was a 190 mph car. They call this AC3 a 1965 GTO even though Ferrari didn't make a GTO in '65. If they had, that's what it would have looked like because Bizzarrini is the one who designed the '62, '63, and '64 GTOs.

The Cobra is a Southern California car with definite hot-rod roots, and this is the very first Cobra built, CSX2001, Shelby's prototype. Every time I drive it, I get a deep emotional rush. My car was the first Cobra ever to race, and it was the only Cobra ever to race in the Tour Auto in France. The body and chassis came from Europe, but it was built in the United States. Its first race was in the States, then it was shipped to France. It did the Le Mans trials but never raced it. It would go on to race for three years in France and Europe. I repatriated the car to the States about fifteen years ago.

I think a love of racing is in your DNA. I started getting into it from the age of thirteen, first with scooters, then motorcycles. By the time I was in my late teens, I was racing motorcycles. My parents didn't know I had motorcycles until I was in my early twenties. For my parents, thinking about cars was a waste of time. Cars were just for transportation. My parents were products of the Depression,

and their parents couldn't afford cars. When I went off to college, my parents purged my room of anything car-related because they figured I'd outgrow my obsession. Just the opposite. A love of cars is part of my makeup.

I don't consider myself a collector; I'm an enthusiast. And I still don't call what I have a "collection." There's one common thread running through the cars I have, and that's me: they embody all the stuff I like. Almost all of my cars have found me. Some of my cars are strictly track, but I would say that 95 percent of them I can drive on the street. I'm taking the Cobra out this weekend, actually. I get great pleasure from the process of preparing it, starting it, driving it, sharing it. Whether it's a watch or a painting or an automobile, the primary motivation of owning it should be that you love it. That's the important thing.

ED BURNS

ACTOR, WRITER & DIRECTOR

—— †† ——

1969 OLDSMOBILE CUTLASS SUPREME

When I was growing up, we had two car guys on my block: one guy's out in his driveway working on his El Camino every weekend, more of a gearhead; the other guy had a '71 Malibu that was just mint, and he was always out front waxing it. Having those two guys and those two cars around, my friends and I became kind of obsessed with the idea of someday becoming a version of those guys. Any friend of ours who had a poster in their room of a Ferrari or a Lamborghini was mocked. That wasn't our thing at all. We never aspired to that.

When I was in high school, I pumped gas at an Exxon station in my town of Valley Stream, New York. Gearheads worked there, hung out there. This was in '85, '86, my junior and senior years. Muscle cars were coming in constantly. That's when I fell in love with the idea of getting one of those classic American muscle cars when I had enough money.

So one day I'm pumping gas. Some guy comes in with a seventies Buick Skylark. Beat to shit, dented driver's window, missing the front bumper—but it's got a For Sale sign in the window. I talk to the guy and get it for 650 bucks after some negotiation. It was a convertible, 350 engine. I got a new door for it, picked up a new bumper from the junkyard.

Going into my senior year, I thought I had a pretty sweet ride.

It wasn't feasible for me to bring that car to college. It never ran well in the winter, and I wasn't enough of a gearhead to keep it running. Going into my sophomore year, I sold it to my cousin for 500 bucks. He sold it within six months. So that was the end of the Skylark. I always regretted selling it. I wish I had just left it in my parents' driveway.

After *Saving Private Ryan*, when I finally made some money, I was determined to buy another Skylark, although I realized that it wasn't exactly what I was looking for—I think the car we all wanted back then was the 442. Either that or the Chevelle Super Sport. I had a friend of mine, a mechanic, helping with the search. We looked all summer long and couldn't find one in good enough shape for what I wanted to spend. Which was not a lot. I wasn't looking to drop fifty grand on a car or anything like that.

Later, my friend Matty and I are going around every used car lot and consignment shop in the Tristate area. In New Jersey, we find a guy who runs a shop, tell him what we're looking for, and he says, "We just got an old automobile in a couple of weeks ago. It's under a tarp in the back lot."

We go back, pull up the tarp, take a look. The car's got four flat tires, a red carpet, and a white roof. Doesn't look like much. Then Matty pops the hood, takes one look at the engine, slams the hood back down, and says to me, "You're going to offer this guy seven grand in cash because he doesn't know what he has and we have to get it off the lot right now." The engine was pristine.

The backstory was apparently that a woman put the car on the lot after her divorce. Her husband had fully restored his-and-hers Cutlass Supremes. They get divorced a year later. She wants to get rid of the car, drops it off at this lot, and it sat there for, I guess, a couple of weeks before we showed up.

We take the car to Matty's shop, and after he's done with it, it's a gorgeous '69, beautiful paint job, cleaned-up interior.

I always aspired to be like the dudes in my neighborhood. I wanted to be the guy who could work on his car, do the restoration himself. Those were badass dudes, and the girls seemed to date those guys. At seventeen, you're all about your car.

PAOLO TUMMINELLI

CAR DESIGN HISTORIAN & PROFESSOR, UNIVERSITY OF COLOGNE

————— || —————

1982 FIAT PANDA 30

You could say I have cars in my DNA. My grandmother raced the Mille Miglia, the Stella Alpina, the Coppa Milano-Sanremo, and all those contests in the fifties, driving Zagatos and Giuliettas. She was the first person to put a steering wheel in my hands, when I was three years old, sitting on her lap in a Citroën DS. The first thing I drew when I was a kid wasn't a house or a dog; it was a car.

I'm a car design historian, a design commentator. My business is consumer culture, which is something I research at the University of Cologne. I'm someone who loves cars and also criticizes cars.

The Panda was not the car I dreamed of when I was fifteen. I was decadent in the extreme; the poster car was a Jaguar XK120, and I also wanted a Rolls-Royce Camargue. I liked British and old-fashioned. Then I studied architecture and design, and I came to understand different values.

I started to consider the Panda in 2007 at a big exhibition at the Museum of Contemporary Art in Rovereto, called "Mito Macchina" in Italian and "Legends of the Open Road" in English. I was on the consulting committee, and there were seventy cars there—Ferraris, Maseratis, Rolls-Royces. There was a Panda, but it was a mock-up model, not a real car. I asked why and I was told, "Well, nobody has a Panda available. Fiat doesn't have a Panda; Italdesign doesn't have a Panda." This was when I first had the sense that we were in danger of losing something.

The Fiat Cinquecento was a symbol of the Italian economic boom of the fifties and sixties, but the Panda, which has the same engine, was more of a transitional product before the marketing and branding era of the nineties. Over time, the Panda was forgotten, thrown away. Yes, the first series was designed by Giorgetto Giugiaro, one of the most prolific Italian car designers, but it was ignored by the car community even though it had sold 4.4 million models. I thought, *You know what? I'll search for one. I'll buy one. I think it's worthwhile.* But I couldn't find one. They were gone.

Eventually I met the editor of *Quattroruote*, the legendary Italian car magazine, and I told him the story: there are no Pandas to buy. He says, "We'll help you find one. We'll make a page saying, 'Paolo Tumminelli would like to have a Panda.'" And they did, and two Pandas popped up, out of 4.4 million.

I flew to Sardinia and purchased a wrecked Panda, drivable but almost completely rotted

TO · 59291L

away. But it took me from Sardinia to Germany—
Olbia to Stuttgart. The exhaust was gone, it was
raining inside the car, the alternator failed, but
it got me to my destination. By this point, I had
started to fall in love with the car. I've owned
Porsches and Mercedes, but I fell in love with a
45-horsepower washing machine on wheels going
neeeeeeeee on the highway. Suddenly you understand the power and mystery of design.

In the end, I needed a replacement. It took
three years to find this one. Can you imagine?
Three years. If you want a Mercedes 300SL, you
make two phone calls and you have five cars to
choose from. You want a Panda? Nothing available.

I stalked the internet every day. Then I saw an
ad, difficult to understand. A Panda 30, the smaller
displacement engine, white, 1982, seven hundred
euros. I called the owner: "Are you sure it's a 1982?
Does the car have a white metal grille, not plastic?" because the first series models by Giugiaro
have metal grilles. He checked for me; the grille
was metal. I said, "I want that car," and I flew to
Torino and bought it.

This is a Fiat Panda 30, which means 30 horsepower, from 1982, designed by Giugiaro. It has
the very rare *tetto apribile* option, a convertible

roof with a double canvas top. Fiat introduced the open-roof option in October 1982, and—funnily enough—nobody ordered it because it was almost winter! Then, in the spring of 1983, they announced that the Panda would be restyled. The *tetto apribile* option remained popular, but not for this original Giugiaro design.

This was a car that had been used for almost thirty years out on the streets, but it was a first series Panda in white, which is actually the color of the mock-up model done by Giugiaro and shown at the exhibition in Rovereto, and with the *tetto apribile*. I bought the car, fixed it mechanically, and had a black-market paint job done by a bodywork specialist who used to work for Officine Meccaniche, in Brescia. The cars back then were painted with nitro paint, very caustic. I had him restore the paint on that car like you would restore an old painting, spot by spot. When I saw the car when it was finished, I almost cried it was so beautiful.

Some cars are meant to be a show-off piece, a sex symbol or a status symbol. The Panda is not that. It has an intrinsic beauty, but you cannot call it a beautiful car. It's a car designed for people to use. You can use it as a truck; you can use it as a city car, for highway driving, whatever you want. It's a practical car, a utilitarian car. It's lightweight, nimble. It does nothing wrong.

Suddenly I understood that it's so much cooler to drive a car like that than any Porsche, Mercedes, Audi, or BMW. You have the cheapest, smallest, dumbest car out there—but nobody has one. I've owned this car for ten years and have never seen another one. Do you know how many Porsches I see every day?

I do own other cars, but I find myself a happier man when I drive the Panda.

LARRY KISS

(WITH BARBARA KISS)

CHECKER CAB ENTHUSIAST

—⊩—

1981 CHECKER A11

BARBARA KISS: It's a real taxi.

LARRY KISS: It was originally ordered in September 1981 by the Poughkeepsie Cab Company. They bought twelve of them. At some point, it made its way to Chelsea, Massachusetts, which is what's on the door. The story we got with it was that it was held as a spare car.

It was very lightly used. It was sold to a gentleman by the name of Steve Contarino, who's a big Checker collector in Haverhill, Massachusetts. We saw it for sale on his website.

BK: Larry has always liked low-production cars, unusual ones. I don't know; we just got hooked. We became like celebrities. People would take our picture.

LK: I always liked to drive something that nobody else has, something different. When the time came to look for a car—this would be back around 2007, 2008, when I was retiring—I thought, *What could I get that I would really enjoy driving?* It came down to the Checker or the Jeep Grand Wagoneer because they both have a nice high seating position. You slide in, you slide out.

I've always been fascinated with old cars and preferred the cars in the back of car lots, normally the least desirable ones. I grew up in Brooklyn. My grandfather had a car, but my family didn't.

BK: Your father didn't drive.

LK: Right. We had the subway nearby.

BK: But you've always had an antique car.

LK: The thing about an antique car, it's a tangible link to the past. You can feel it. You can sit in it. You can close your eyes and be back again in whatever time you're thinking of. The beauty of a Checker as opposed to all other cars is that it resonates with people who have no interest in cars. They know what it is right away.

BK: Mostly, it's children riding on those huge seats. We get a lot of that.

LK: Or someone will say, "That's the first car I rode in when I arrived at Kennedy Airport in America. I was five years old, and it took me to my new home. I'll never forget that." They remember it forty years later.

BK: Or you get a cabdriver remembering how thirteen new arrivals and all their luggage fit into the Checker at the same time.

LK: In American history, every immigrant group that settled in New York drove cabs. They worked hard, maybe bought a medallion, and that medallion financed their homes, college for their kids.

I heard an interesting take on that story recently. This guy, a lawyer, says, "I'm in a very, very powerful practice in the city. All the senior partners drove Checker taxis in college during the sixties and seventies. They love to tell stories. And proudly mounted in all their offices, right next to their law degrees, are their hack licenses, with a picture of them when they were twenty-one."

BK: Well, you still tell the stories.

LK: Yes. I drove a cab for a very short while.

BK: Briefly.

LK: Every group has gone into the taxi industry.

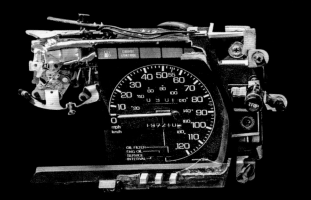

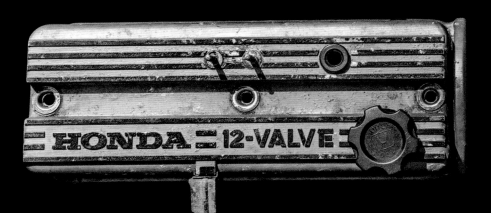

BRIAN GARRITY

LAWYER

———— H ————

1985 HONDA ACCORD (FORMERLY)

My dad bought this car, his first new-car purchase, with his girlfriend, who helped him pick out the color (Champagne Beige Metallic—a really pretentious way of saying *beige*). A few years later, she would become his wife, and a few years after that, they had me.

About ten years later, he sold the car to his brother, my godfather, John (he sold it for either one dollar or two hundred dollars—the details are murky). And less than a year after that, he was diagnosed with lung cancer. When he passed away in March 1998, I was nine years old, the oldest of three children.

When my dad was alive, his brothers were at our house every weekend, helping him with his many home-renovation projects. After he passed, though, they became increasingly distant. It turns out that as I grew up and began exhibiting my dad's mannerisms and physical attributes and even hints of his deep, booming voice, the increasing resemblance proved too painful a reminder for them to bear.

When I was old enough to start thinking about what I would drive when I earned my license, I asked my godfather what had happened to my dad's old Accord. Somewhat poetically, the car had died shortly after my father had, and it had to be taken off the road. But my godfather still had it— probably not for any sentimental reasons, since he still has a fully built Volkswagen Beetle engine his friend had overbored back in the seventies. When I offered to buy the Honda from him, he made me a counteroffer: If I paid for all the parts and woke up early every Saturday morning, he'd work with me to get it running again. He said, "I'm thinking it will take you a thousand dollars. We put a few months' work into it and get it back on the road. We do that, it's yours."

About four years and five thousand dollars later, I had my first car. As with most car projects' estimates, my godfather's had been overly optimistic. But I don't regret a second or a penny spent: that car would help my family move into two different houses and be involved in most of my favorite high school memories, and it brought my dad's brothers back into my family's orbit. Those early Saturday mornings and late nights taught me so much, not only about cars but also about my dad. My godfather would tell me stories about him growing up in Paterson, New Jersey—the type of stories I never thought I'd hear without my dad around to tell them.

After surviving seven months of adventures in high school, the Accord was involved in a hit-and-run while parked; the impact drove it back 5 feet and ripped out a quarter panel and most of the headlights. It powered on for one more month before succumbing to the damage.

Since the car couldn't make it to college with me, my mom, bless her heart and patience, let this eyesore stay parked at her house (probably driving down property values) for all of my four years of college. Despite many attempts to get it running again, it couldn't be resurrected.

A year after school, rather than let what had been my dad's first brand-new car, and my first car ever, go silently and unceremoniously into that good night, I invited a few close friends—most of whom had shared some of the countless memorable experiences I'd had in the Accord—to help me pay my respects. It had been a rough year for us, and the old car gave us one last gift: hours of blowing off a year's worth of stress using a sledge-hammer and a few baseball bats.

I still can't believe that my mom not only let us do this in her driveway, the same driveway where the car had sat for five years, but also took a ton of pictures and videos to document that day. It was just an absolutely crazy scene. More than five years later, I don't think I've ever had more fun.

AFSHIN BEHNIA

FOUNDER, PETROLICIOUS

———H———

1965 ALFA ROMEO GIULIA SS

Most people seem to fall in love with the cars they admired during their teen years, which for me would be the cars from the early to mid-eighties. I like those for sure, but I was always more drawn to the design of European cars from the fifties, sixties, and seventies.

I have a vivid memory of the first time I fell in love with a car. I was four years old, and my mom got a brand-new BMW 2002. It was mint green, just gorgeous. My mom drove it aggressively, and I loved the sound of it. That 2002 made me curious about cars and also made me appreciate them.

When I was twenty, I got a 1986 Alfa Romeo Spider. At the time, it was just a used car, not really a collectible, but I thought it would be fun to have. I owned it for maybe three years. I didn't buy another Alfa until 2008, when I got this Giulia SS. I believe that you don't choose the Alfa; the Alfa chooses you. At first, I bought into the usual stereotypes about Alfa: it's Italian, so it's probably not reliable, or it's not going to be as good a driver as a BMW. But all of that proved to be wrong. It's fantastic to drive and really advanced for its time, engineering-wise.

Since 2008, I've bought a few Alfas that needed a lot of care or even a total restoration. Each time I saw one in this state, I felt bad that such a nice piece of machinery was going to be neglected or thrown away, so I had to save it.

I never envisioned myself to be a one-marque sort of person. It just happened that way. If you'd asked me fifteen years ago, "How do you envision your dream garage?" I would have said it would be very eclectic, with all kinds of models from all different periods. But after the first Alfa, then the second one, then the third, I just wanted all different flavors of Alfas—different eras, different body shells. It's like going down the rabbit hole.

I think some of the new high-performance electric cars could be appreciated in the future like vintage cars are today. It won't be the technology that will determine that, though; it will be how well the car is executed. Was it designed to be a pure appliance? If so, no one will care about it in thirty years. But if it's a model with character, built for a specific type of driver in mind, then I think it stands a good chance of becoming a classic.

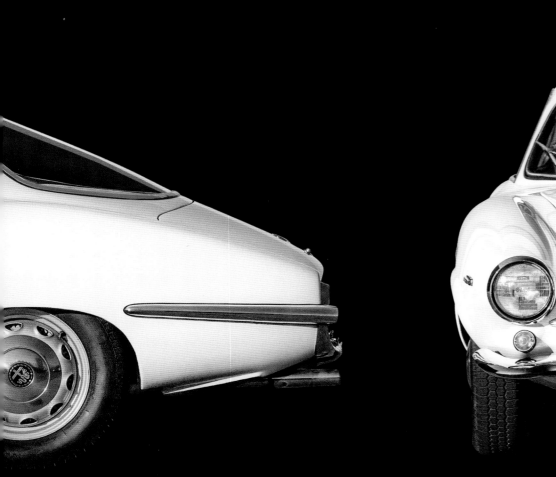

FRANZ VON HOLZHAUSEN

CHIEF DESIGNER, TESLA

—⊣⊢—

TESLA MODEL S PROTOTYPE

My mom says she has a picture of me when I was two, sitting in a high chair and drawing a car. I think it starts there.

I grew up in a household of design. My father started a practice right around the time I was born, a product and graphics design consulting business. In the early years, he operated the business out of our basement, so I could hang out and learn, just explore what it all meant.

My dad loved cars. He always had Porsches around—Porsche 911s, the 924, and, when it came out, the 944. He had Mustangs, too. He always had a fun car around.

I went to Syracuse University but spent only two years there. My father was a Syracuse graduate; I had some of the same professors he had. He was the president of the East Coast Industrial Designers Society of America, and one evening he called me up while I was sitting in my dorm room, probably freezing my ass off. He was at ArtCenter, in Pasadena, for some conference, and he said, "You've got to get out here and see this place." I jumped on a plane and met him there, did the tour, saw the school. They were like, "Look, you can come, but you'll be really young. Why don't you get a couple of years under your belt and then come back." Two years later, I signed up on the spot, drove my Volkswagen GTI across the country, and started at ArtCenter at the end of the summer. That was when I realized that you could actually put the two—a passion for cars, and a passion for design—together and make a living doing that.

ArtCenter opened my eyes and connected me with the industry in ways I don't think would have been possible through most other programs. ArtCenter had a sister school in Switzerland, so I went there. I had internships at VW and Ford, where I learned so much about the realities of being a car designer—the business, the industry, what it takes.

I joined Tesla in August 2008. I sat down with Elon Musk to figure out what the attributes of the Model S really should be. We realized that if Tesla was going to be successful, we had to create a strong foundation to build on: this was going to be the first fully designed and engineered vehicle that Tesla would produce.

We took a very clean sheet of paper, like an author sitting down and thinking, *Okay, I need to write a novel, and it needs to have these elements in it*. That moment of staring at the blank page, thinking, *Where do I even start?* There was

that pressure like, *If we don't succeed, we close the shop.*

Elon for sure had a vision of what he wanted to accomplish. We knew it needed to be a credible product that could beat an internal-combustion-engine vehicle at every level. The skeleton was built on some key attributes: general size, what our performance characteristics needed to be, what the range needed to be, what the interior volumes should hold, how many passengers. From there, it was really about taking a bunch of adjectives and turning them into a product.

From the early moments, I realized that we needed a theme around which to galvanize the product. Tesla's story is really about efficiency through and through, and that became the underlying theme for the car: everything we did was focused around efficiency. Everything tied back to this word.

The early Model S inspiration came from a tuned athlete, because a high-level athlete is, in a way, tuning their whole lifestyle—their regimen, their nutrition—toward efficiency. Everything is geared toward efficiency, and toward the ultimate goal of winning at whatever level.

We were able to create something that captured all the desired elements: the lowest aerodynamic coefficient of drag of any sedan at the time; nimbleness, with excellent performance; the ability to accelerate to 60 mph in under five seconds, which was pretty quick. And it had great range and looked modern without being strange or quirky.

I think the Model S has proven itself to be a game changer—iconic, still an incredibly relevant vehicle on the road right now. We were able to captivate the imagination, to inspire people to join our mission of a clean-energy transportation solution with a product that doesn't make them feel like they're sacrificing something. It still looks modern, sexy—timeless. You can't pinpoint its era. It's a sweet-spot recipe.

ALEXANDER KRAFT

CEO, SOTHEBY'S
INTERNATIONAL REALTY FRANCE

—— †† ——

**1968 FERRARI 365 GT 2+2 &
1993 RANGE ROVER
CLASSIC VOGUE LSE**

I've always been a car nut. My uncle had a 911S, and there's a photo of me sitting on the hood when I was three years old.

When I was young, my father bought me a shitty twenty-year-old Ford Fiesta—a real rust bucket. He said, "If you want to get it in shape, go to the local garage and they'll teach you how to fix a car." The mechanics showed me how to do an oil change, how to replace spark plugs, even how to weld.

I've always especially loved vintage cars. For me, they're not so much cars as objects of beauty, especially with the effects of time—aged leather, old wood, the smell of oil. I wanted to own a vintage car as soon as I could. I bought my first one when I was at Cambridge: an MG Midget. I was a very happy guy, zipping around Cambridge in that old MG.

I've had a lot of classic cars over the years, and many were very rare. But vintage cars are usually disappointing to drive. For example, my beloved, beautiful Porsche 356 had more or less a VW Beetle engine, 90 horsepower, tiny wheels. Impossible to drive these days. It looked like a sports car but didn't feel like one. After a while, my philosophy changed and I thought, *I like bespoke suits and bespoke shoes—why not make bespoke cars?*

I had an upgraded Jaguar XK150 for seven or eight years—air-conditioning from an E-Type, electric steering, bigger discs, brake system. I enjoyed it, but I wanted something else.

I started looking for 250, 330, and 365 GT 2+2 models. The only Ferraris that really appeal to me are those big GTs from the fifties and sixties, the cars an Onassis or a Niarchos, one of the industrialist playboys, would have driven. Then this car popped up at a London dealer. I noticed it had a V12 engine, as it should have, but it wasn't a Ferrari engine; it was a Jaguar engine. I called the dealer the next day, and he told me that the car had been used as a donor car, for the motor, by a Ferrari replica specialist in New Zealand. The first owner had actually been Greg Garrison, a TV producer and a Ferrari collector. The car was built to European specifications but sold new in California, originally in an aubergine color.

I bought the car because the engine was not original. For many people, that would have been a turnoff, but it meant I could do what I wanted to the car without committing what would have been sacrilege to purists. I had the license to put my own stamp on it.

1968 FERRARI 365 GT 2+2

I was in the shop one day as the mechanics were preparing to apply new paint, stripping the car down to bare metal, and I saw it for the first time without bumpers. It was a real "Hallelujah!" moment. I thought, *Wow, that car looks so sexy.* So much better than with the bumpers, which disfigure the car. I also took out the chrome frame around the rear lights, and took out the nonfunctional reflector and just kept the two round lights, and all of a sudden, it looked almost like a GTB.

It had the original upholstery, which was actually vinyl. I decked it out with real Ferrari cognac leather. But it still had the plastic dashboard and plastic tunnel, and that didn't look right to me, even though that's how Ferrari built it. So I thought, *Let's cover them in leather.* Again, not something for the purist, but I think that's what the designers at Ferrari or Pininfarina would have done back then if they could have.

At one point, I thought hard about trying to find another Ferrari engine—but even if I had, it wouldn't have had matching numbers, so what would have been the point? The mechanics at my garage said, "Listen, you've got a really good V12 engine, one of the best in the world, and it's period-correct. Why not just tinker with it?" So we installed a bespoke fuel-injection system to channel all that power, make it more reliable. And we transformed it aesthetically to look more like a Ferrari competition engine from the fifties or sixties, painting parts of it red and adding air floaters to look like those famous trumpets. It looks correct and it feels correct, but it's almost better than the original because now I get 300 horsepower—much more than the original engine. It's a V12 with great sound that goes like hell and is very reliable. It's almost a daily driver now.

The 1993 Range Rover was another car I knew I could make my own. At that time, SUVs were utilitarian, and the Range Rover was the first luxury SUV. The queen had one; all the big shots from the seventies through the nineties had one. I just love that car.

I did a complete bare-metal respray and restored the leather—but what I had always dreamed of was a bespoke trunk. I had seen some examples in the later Holland & Holland editions, some Overfinch customizations, but I wanted to take it even further. The trunk I had made almost looks like it belongs on a boat: beautiful wood, ten layers of clear varnish. Like in the Holland models, I had a gun drawer put in, because I love clay shooting. I also put in a humidor and a travel bar, because you always need a bar, right? I had always dreamed of having a working espresso machine in a car. These guys in Monaco, LH Corporation, came up with a solution: they put in an espresso machine, gave it its own power supply, and converted it to 12 volts, and it's fully working.

For me, getting from A to Z is probably the least important thing about cars. Getting there is a by-product of the restoration process. Cars are things of beauty; they tell a story. I'm interested in savoir faire, in know-how, in doing things and creating things, especially with gifted artisans. I'm always looking forward to the next project.

PETER KALIKOW

REAL ESTATE DEVELOPER

———— ‖ ————

1973 MIRAGE

My love affair with automobiles started when I was fifteen and saw a Ferrari for the first time at the New York Car Show in 1958. Fast-forward to 1969, when I had this crazy idea to make my own car. There's a great scene in the movie *Grand Prix*; a guy is asked about race driving, "Do you ever get afraid?" He replies, "If I ever thought about the idea of going into a wall at 150 miles an hour, I would stop racing. I guess it's a lack of imagination that makes me race." I find that sentiment to be exactly on point because I didn't know how hard it was going to be to build the car I wanted—a full four-seat luxury car with world-class handling and acceleration. It didn't exist.

There were some things that were just lacking in the American market. Bentleys were too expensive, and they had a bad image, at least with people my age. The real competition was Aston Martin. That was my goal, to build a better Aston Martin. My plan was to take the bodies off Camaros, modify the rear suspensions, and put a five-speed transmission in them. There were issues that I thought I could make better. And things that Americans liked that the Europeans just didn't do. The Italians never finished under the dashboards, for example. I thought there was room in

the market for me, especially since I was thinking about making only fifty cars a year.

I went to Italy, got a guided tour of the Ferrari works. Same with Maserati. That's where I met Giulio Alfieri, the chief engineer there. He told me I couldn't build the car I wanted off a Camaro chassis. I asked why not, and he said, "You make fifty cars, you make fifty enemies." I needed to build a car from the ground up.

So Alfieri got permission from the owner of Maserati to design a brand-new car. The chassis was all ours. The car could fit four people, with a full trunk to hold golf clubs and bags, something Ferraris didn't have; there was no trunk space in a Ferrari. The wheels were made for me by Campagnolo, which was an up-and-coming company. People were starting to get away from wire wheels. These were actually cast as an alloy with aluminum and magnesium.

The prototype was made on a buck, and then that became a manufacturing model. We were going to make twelve cars on the buck. The next batch of body parts would have been made by a company that would stamp them out for us. The problem was, I wanted to retail the car for thirteen thousand dollars, which was less than Astons,

1973 MIRAGE

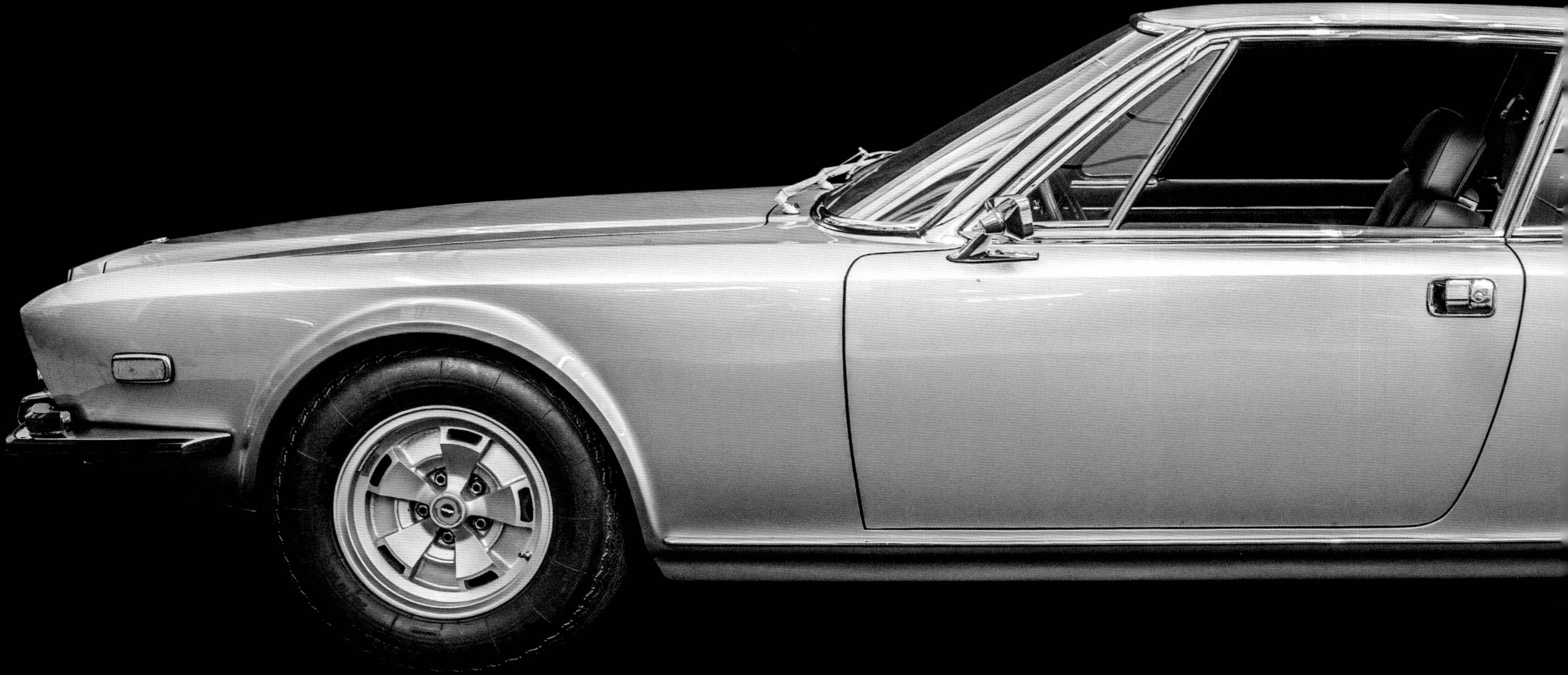

Ferraris, and Maseratis. I wasn't sure about the financial viability, but by the time I started having doubts, we were already in the process of making six cars.

When we did all the analysis, we realized that we would have had to retail the cars for twenty thousand dollars to break even. But people loved the car. Maybe they liked the price; I don't know.

We decided to call it the Mirage after a famous French air force fighter plane. It was the best plane the Israeli Air Force used during the Six-Day War. But my lawyer said I couldn't use the name because it was a copyright issue, and we'd get in trouble with the manufacturer who made the planes. I told him, "Don't give me shit. I read the copyright law. I'm not even a lawyer, but I read it." In the end, this was a car, so they weren't even in the same field. I liked the name, so we kept it.

PETERSEN AUTOMOTIVE MUSEUM

The Petersen Automotive Museum in Los Angeles is a beautifully curated space. Thanks to having received an introduction to one of the museum's directors, I was lucky enough to spend time in its basement, where they keep their archive of vehicles and materials that have been either purchased by or donated to the museum.

There was so much to take in, I tried to focus only on the vehicles that spoke to me—the ones I had some connection with because of what they represented, their design, or their famous owners. For those reasons, I chose to include the Ferrari from *Magnum, P.I.*; the DeLorean; Elvis's Pantera (he shot the steering wheel!); and Steve McQueen's Jaguar. Each of these cars had an impact on me when I was growing up.

1982 FERRARI 308 GTSI "MAGNUM, P.I."

Tom Selleck drove this car during the 1982–83 season
of the television series *Magnum, P.I.* The padding was
removed from the driver's seat so that 6-foot-4 Selleck
could drive the car comfortably. This Spider model, or
S version, has a removable roof panel for a better view
of the interior and of the actor.

1980 DELOREAN DMC-12 "GOLD PLATED"

This special-edition DeLorean DMC-12 was sold through the 1980 American Express catalog exclusively to Gold Card members for $85,000 (more than $250,000 today). Aside from its 24-karat-gold-plated stainless-steel body, it was otherwise identical to standard models. One hundred gold models were planned for production, but only five were sold.

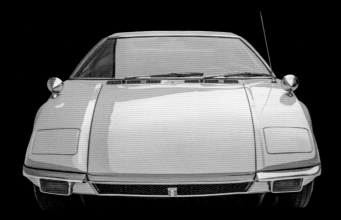

1971 DE TOMASO PANTERA "ELVIS PRESLEY"

Elvis Presley purchased this car in 1974 as a gift for his then-girlfriend, Linda Thompson. Following an argument with Thompson, Presley tried to take off in the car, but it wouldn't start. So he jumped out of the car, pulled out a pistol, and fired three rounds into the interior. The resulting bullet holes—two in the steering wheel and one in the driver's-side floor pan—are still visible today.

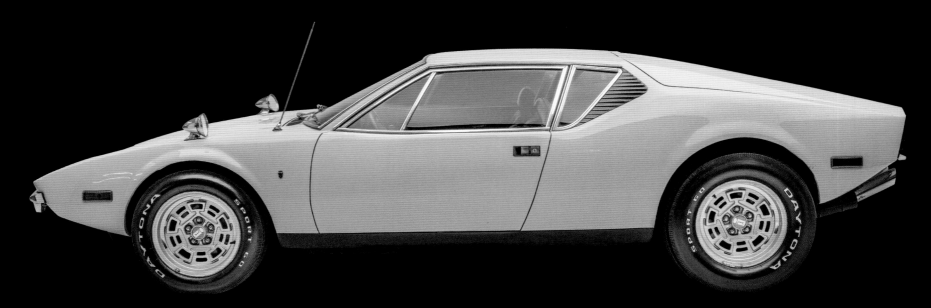

1956 JAGUAR XKSS

This race-bred Jaguar was Steve McQueen's favorite car. The XKSS was one of the fastest road-legal cars available at the time, and he enjoyed driving it fast, especially on the streets of LA, accumulating so many speeding tickets that his license was almost suspended. Originally the car was white with a red interior, but McQueen had it repainted British racing green and retrimmed with black leather upholstery.

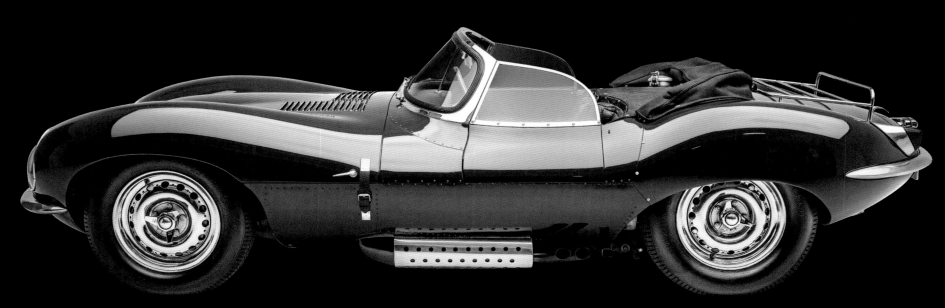

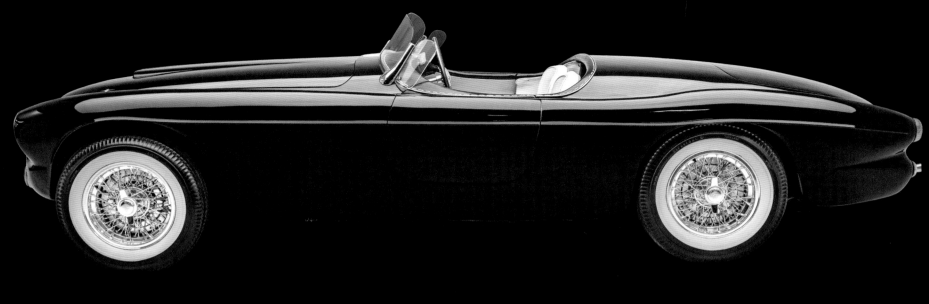

1952 FERRARI 212/225 INTER BARCHETTA BY CARROZZERIA TOURING SUPERLEGGERA

This particular Ferrari, the final nonracing Ferrari to be bodied by legendary automobile coachbuilder Carrozzeria Touring, was gifted to Henry Ford II by Enzo Ferrari himself. To appeal to the American audience, the car was fitted with the more powerful 225-horsepower engine and whitewall tires. This was Ford's personal car until he donated it to the Ford design studio. It was also the inspiration behind the 1955 Ford Thunderbird.

1932 FORD "RAY BROWN ROADSTER"

In 1945 and early 1946, seventeen-year-old Ray Brown built this roadster while working for Eddie Meyer Engineering Company in Hollywood, California. He painted the hot rod Sherwood Green, a distinctive 1946 Buick color. In 1948, Ray sold the car, after which it was put in dry storage for nearly forty years. In 1991, it was discovered in untouched original condition, complete with eleven timing tags. Following a ground-up restoration that returned the car to its original racing configuration, it has won multiple awards.

ESTEBAN URIETA

TESLA DESIGN STUDIO MASTER MODELER

—————H—————

1961 CHEVY IMPALA

I grew up in Orange County, California, in the city of Fullerton. In my neighborhood, there were a lot of lowriders. Since I was a little kid, that was a thing for me. But it takes a lot of money and time to build one. I never thought that someday I would own one myself.

I started out building model cars. From the model cars, I jumped to lowrider bikes. From the lowrider bikes, I jumped into the cars. At first it was G-bodies: '82, '85 Buick Regals; Monte Carlos. In the '90s, Nissan trucks, too—they were popping a lot. I was doing mini truckin', also.

I'm a fabricator, working in the car industry for more than twenty-five years. I build cars from scratch. I know metal, I know upholstery, I know interior. Paint, electrical, mechanical—everything. It started with an '82 Regal. I fixed it up, not to top-of-the-line, like this Impala, but it had hydraulics, a sound system, rims. I sold it, made a little bit off that car because I did most of the work.

After I sold my Regal, I bought a 1965 Impala. That was my first classic car. After that, a '49 Fleetline—they call them Bombs. Then I was getting married and needed money, so I sold all my cars and bought a Honda Civic, just for work. It was a big sacrifice. My wife knew I basically gave it all up for her. But I always knew that I was going to get another car later on.

When I bought this car and had the keys in my hand, it was a profound experience. Looking at it, knowing it was mine, that I was the owner, I felt chills run through my body.

This one wasn't stock. It had hydraulics already, and it was painted. I started putting my touch on the car, all the engraving. Basically, it's just detail after detail after detail.

Engraving in LA County started, I would say, in the early 2000s. You didn't see it much, because it's really expensive. First you have to polish the metal. After you polish it, you do all the engraving. Then you dip it in copper, polish it again. Then dip it in chrome.

I didn't want to go crazy on the car. Just to do little things as accents. I started with the mirrors. Then the door handles. Then the base for the antenna, the tailpipes, all the exhaust, everything—all hand-engraved. Once you finish a car, you take it to a show. I put it up on jack stands, put mirrors on the floor, and lights so people can actually see all the detail in the car. In the end, all the hard work and time that go into the car pay off because everyone loves it, too.

"When I bought this car and had the keys in my hand, it was a profound experience. Looking at it, knowing it was mine, that I was the owner, I felt chills run through my body."

—ESTEBAN URIETA

NIXON HRANEK

SEVEN-YEAR-OLD

——— ‖ ———

CUSTOM-BUILT
TOY LAND ROVER

What I like most about my truck is that it can drive and it has keys. And I can open the back and climb in there. If I could change the truck, I would want it to have music and maybe be green. And have doors that open! If the truck had music, I would play "Bounce It" by Juicy J.

I like cars because they have cool wheels. My car has a tire on the front, and if my tire breaks, I can put another one on!

I like to drive on the grass because it's a truck. Sometimes driving the car, I feel scared. I like driving with my sister, Harlow, because she's safer.

When I get older, I want a Lamborghini. The red one, like in *Dumb and Dumber*.

KEVIN COSTNER

ACTOR & PRODUCER

———— H ————

1968 SHELBY MUSTANG GT350 CONVERTIBLE

We were filming *Bull Durham*, and this was the car that the director/screenwriter, Ron Shelton, identified my character as having, which I think was a really solid choice. It was a car a rogue would have—this guy in the minor leagues on the East Coast with a quintessential California car. It just fit him so perfectly.

It was red, but it was rusted out, almost a primer gray. I became really fond of it. When the movie was over, it meant so much to me, I wanted to buy it, so I went to the producer. I think the production company had bought it for fourteen thousand dollars and put four thousand into it to make it right for the movie. So I was prepared to buy it for the eighteen thousand, but this producer wanted twenty-one thousand.

I thought, *That's fine. It's still a part of me. I still want it.* It was unusual that I would even do that, because I'm not a car guy. But I bought it, and brought it back home and refurbished it, put a great paint job on it. I just love driving it.

It's impossible to take your eyes off that car. People on the freeway look at it—guys really look at it hard. It's just one of those cars that you can put next to the most expensive car on the road and it will stand out.

I keep stuff from my movies. I have the bow from *Robin Hood*. I have my guns from *Wyatt Earp*. I bought the Ford from *The Highwaymen*, the car that chased down Bonnie and Clyde. If I ever put my own memorabilia up for auction, I imagine that Mustang is going to be in there.

PAUL ZUCKERMAN

LAWYER

———— H ————

1966 PORSCHE 911

When I was a kid—it must have been about 1970 or so—my mother took me to pick up the family station wagon from the mechanic. We took a cab, but when we were dropped off, the mechanic hadn't finished the work. There were no cell phones then; if someone said something would be done at a certain time, you showed up as promised—there was no checking in with texts or anything like that. My mother was upset, so the mechanic gave my mother his AMC AMX to use.

That car was loud. It had a Hurst four-speed, and just being in that car—the sound of it, the power of it, seeing the shifter shake in its housing—made me car crazy.

My first car was a 1979 Formula Firebird. This was in 1983 on Long Island, where everybody liked Firebirds. I always liked muscle cars—those were my first love—but I also liked Benzes. I always gravitated toward something old, with some style. I bought a '74 Coupe de Ville, black with a red interior. I was always buying whatever classic car I could get my hands on affordably.

When I started to have some financial wherewithal, I went in the direction of those muscle cars I had lusted after in my youth. I quickly realized that most of those were not drivers. They looked great, they sounded great, and they were exquisite shitboxes. Around that time, I had a neighbor, Spike Feresten, and also a friend, Steve Levy, who were always driving Porsches. I had an image problem with Porsche. I felt that they were rich-kid cars. But seeing how Spike and Steve enjoyed them, I started to overcome my prejudice. I found a guy who had a beautiful '72 RS in Viper Green and bought it, and then I was hooked.

This is a base 911, 1966. That's all they sold for that year. A bit of arcane Porsche history: 1965 was the first regular production year of the 911, but Porsche did not have authorization to sell the 911 in the United States that year. So Porsche had an unusually short '65 model year, and as soon as they could, they declared everything to be a '66. This is a very early car, an October '65 build, around number 2,300 of the 911 model.

This car is unbelievably, astoundingly original, and it's in great condition. The car was discovered by a fellow by the name of Jeff Trask, who unearthed it in Palos Verdes. According to the legend, the original owner bought it new, European delivery. He drove it in Europe, then brought it back to the States, driving it until 1975. That's when the 55 mph national speed limit was instituted.

The owner parked the 911 in his garage in protest. It was cleaned once a month and started once a month and otherwise taken care of, but it sat there until he died in 2012 or 2013.

I drive it sparingly, but this car takes me back in time. It smells like an unrestored car. It smells like an original 911, from the leather to the stuffing to the machinery. It just evokes a car from that age.

Sometimes I think, *Okay, I'm in a '66.* My father, a first-generation American who came from very poor circumstances, was forty years old in 1966 and was just starting to come into his own. I was a year old when this car was born. LBJ was president; the Vietnam War was escalating. There was no European Union. Germany was starting what they call the economic miracle, and Porsche didn't want to piss off Mercedes by making a car that Mercedes would feel was competing on their turf, because Porsche was so small then, such a lightweight. Then you remember how scary life seemed in the seventies—we were all going to perish. And still I look back and think, *Boy, life was fucking simple then.*

SNOOP DOGG

MULTI-PLATINUM ARTIST, ACTOR, PHILANTHROPIST & ENTERTAINMENT ICON

—————||—————

1965 CADILLAC "SNOOP DE VILLE" CONVERTIBLE

My first car? A four-door Datsun, orange. I used it on the album cover for *Ego Trippin* in front of Long Beach Poly High School. The car on that cover was clean. The motherfucker wasn't like that when I had it.

My inspiration for cars comes from black exploitation movies. I was a fan of Cadillacs, Coupe de Villes. I had put a lyric together called "Snoop De Ville"—this is 2002, the year Willie Mac and the Patriots beat the Rams in the Super Bowl—and I wanted to make my own Cadillac, a better version of it. Cars are man's best friend.

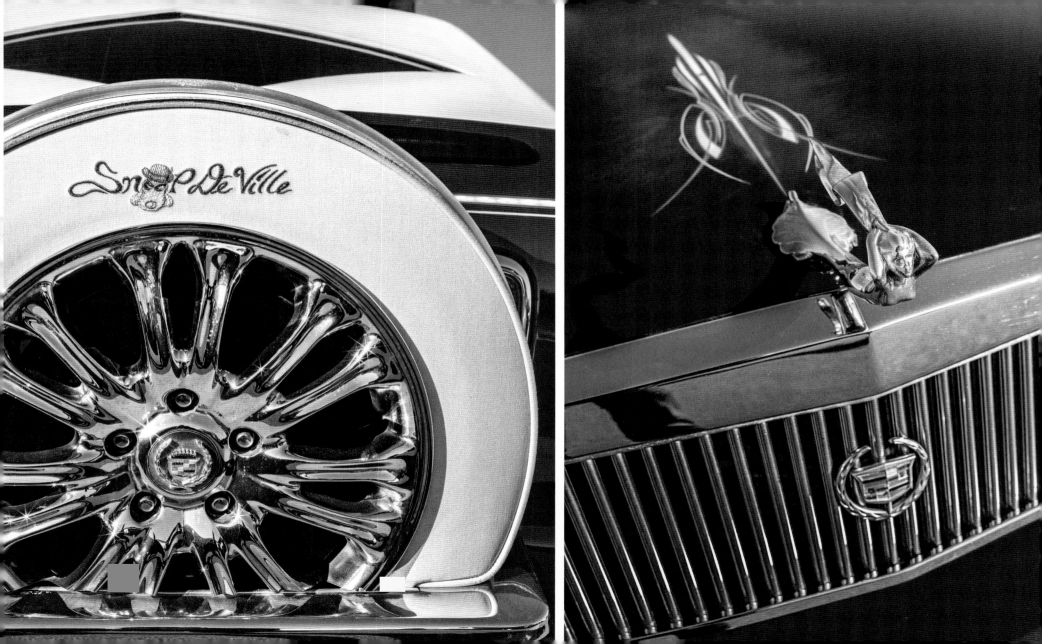

RALPH LAUREN

FASHION DESIGNER

—— ⊢⊦ ——

1971 MERCEDES-BENZ 280SE CABRIOLET

I've owned this car since the day I started Polo. There was a guy backing me with a fifty-thousand-dollar loan to start my business. At that time, I didn't have a car. I thought, *I have a new business; I need a car*. I had admired this Mercedes convertible. So I went to a guy on Park Avenue and said, "I want a silver Mercedes 280SE 3.5, with tan leather seats and a tan canvas top." He said, "No, sir. We make them in black." I said, "No, I want tan leather and I want a tan top." That's what I got.

My partner, who had a 50 percent ownership of the company, said, "You bought a car for *thirteen thousand dollars*?" I didn't have a master plan. I didn't have a car, so I bought a car—that was it. Anyway, I paid him back.

This is just who I am. I've always liked timeless things. Everything I've done, it's never been for a great investment. Any car I've owned or built, it's because I loved it. When I was growing up, I didn't even have a bike. A car to me was a way to represent myself, another form of artistic expression. It's a dream. *Where am I in this car? What's the look?* Just like you get the right tweed jacket, the right jeans, you get the right car for your life.

There's a funny story about this car. I have three kids, and years back—they must have been seven, eight years old—we were out on the beach in Long Island when they decided to wash my car with seawater. They kept dropping rags into the rocks and then using them on the car. They had wrecked it. I had to have the car repainted.

I don't get rid of anything. I have a closet full of clothes that I love but don't know what to do with. There are some cars you begin to love for the beauty, like a painting. You say, *I love that. I'm not going to drive that car, but it's so beautiful, I want to keep it*. Plus, as time goes on, these cars I bought just keep going up in value.

But a car does more than just look the part. It's exciting to drive, to listen to the engine. It's fun, athletic. The car is unique for men. It's sport. It's a way to know you've arrived. The cars you relate to most have a story behind them. And eventually they tell you that story.

"The car is unique for men. It's sport. It's a way to know you've arrived. The cars you relate to most have a story behind them. And eventually they tell you that story."

—RALPH LAUREN

ROD EMORY

FOUNDER, EMORY MOTORSPORTS

———— ‖ ————

1955 PORSCHE 356 "EMORY SPECIAL"

I've been in Porsche racing and restoration as a business for thirty years. But all of this actually started before I was born.

My grandfather was a custom-car builder more than seventy years ago. In the forties and fifties, he had a shop called Valley Custom Shop in Burbank, California—he was one of the pioneers of customizing, chopping, channeling, and sectioning early American hot rods. Then, in 1961, he became the body shop manager at Chick Iverson Volkswagen Porsche, in Newport. A year later, my father, Gary Emory, graduated from high school in North Hollywood and went to work for the same Porsche dealership in the detail department, and then became the Porsche parts manager.

So at this Porsche dealership, my grandfather is running the body shop, and my father is running the parts department. When my mom was pregnant with me, my dad took her to the hospital in a short wheelbase 1965 911. Porsche is in my DNA.

I grew up racing bicycles, motorcycles, three-wheelers, ATVs. I had a dream of one day becoming a race car driver. When I was fourteen, my dad found an old '53 Porsche. We bought it for three thousand dollars, which was real money in '87 or

'88, and I began the restoration of it with my father and grandfather. It took two years and all the skills I had been learning since I was a kid. I modified pretty much everything I could. I lowered it, put fog lights on it, hood straps. I split the windshield into two parts because I wanted it to look like one of the early factory Porsche cars.

It was done in 1990. I got my racing license, had a friend hand-paint the Pegasus horse on the side, put a yellow number 80 and a yellow DUNLOP on the sides of the tires, and went racing.

I raced for a couple of years in that car. After I graduated from high school, I was racing up at the Portland Historics. A young guy comes up to me and says, "I love watching you race. Would you consider building me a car and teaching me how to go race driving?" That was the beginning of Emory Motorsports. From that point until now, that's what we've been doing: building, restoring, and racing vintage Porsches.

For a long time, we were primarily focused on building race cars, finding the performance of the 356. But around ten years after I built my first car, I thought, *I really want to heavily modify one of these cars*—to pull that inspiration from my grandfather and dad, do a true custom car.

In 1997, my wife, Amy, and I began the restoration on this 356. We stripped it down to bare metal and started on all the metalwork. We leaned the windshield back, leaned the nose back, raised the wheel arches. We modified all the suspension, put a special engine in it, rolled the rockers and doors all the way under the floor—gave it some of that Spyder influence. We pulled some inspiration from the Abarth Carrera, adding louvers in the rear and lengthening the tail. That was the Emory Special.

In the middle of that restoration, we found out we were expecting our first child. We had been married for only a couple of years at that point, so when we had our son, we wanted to travel around and see family. We were debuting the car that year in August at Porsche's fiftieth-anniversary event in Monterey, so we put a hitch on the back, restored a little trailer, and in 1998, Amy, our newborn son, Zane, and I set out on a 4,500-mile journey, driving this 356 all around the western United States, from Oregon to Monterey, all through California down to San Diego, back up to Bishop, through Death Valley, and over to Arizona, Nevada, and Utah.

We had one oil line fail us, and while visiting Amy's family, we hit this torrential downpour just south of Salt Lake City. We hadn't anticipated rain, so I hadn't put wipers on the car yet. So we pulled off at the first exit and went to an auto parts store.

The car had all Lexan-type plastic race windows, so we drilled a hole through the windshield, and I figured out how to screw a Ford window crank handle to a wiper blade I bought. For the next fifty or sixty miles, Amy operated the windshield wiper by hand as I drove. Then we continued north, up into Idaho. It was an amazing road tour, just the three of us. To this day, there's still a hole in the windshield with a little rubber plug in it.

The way I see it, cars are either transportation—any brand, any make, any model—or they have a culture that surrounds them. For me, that culture is Porsche. When I was born, I was brought home from the hospital in a Porsche. The first time I got behind the wheel was in a Porsche. I've made a living for thirty years in a Porsche. I took my own son home from the hospital in a Porsche. It's part of my friends and family all over the world. It's not just a car for me. It's life and culture.

STEVE SCHRADER

VP INTERNATIONAL MARKETING, ARCO

———— H ————

1973 JAGUAR E-TYPE V12 CONVERTIBLE

I can remember, in the late 1950s, leaving the dentist's office and seeing a Jaguar XK150 parked on the street. It was the first time I'd ever seen a Jaguar, and the impression of it never left my mind.

In the seventies, I came across an XK120 Roadster that was owned by Edgar Hires, of the Hires root beer family, who called himself "the black sheep of the family." Edgar described buying this XK120 in 1952, in New York City. Right-hand drive, one of the all-aluminum cars, which was really special because Jaguar made only a couple hundred of them. He said, "Steve, I got out of that showroom and drove down Madison Avenue, and the eyes of the world were looking at me." So I bought that car, restored it, came to California, and drove the car until the late eighties, when I got this one.

Jaguar has a very interesting history. Founded in 1922, after World War II they started building roadsters with this brand-new engine, a twin overhead cam six-cylinder. They kept that basic engine design, with some adjustments, for two decades, until 1971, when they came out with the V12, in the E-Type. I knew that at some point, I wanted to get the "new" car with the "new" engine, because I had the previous-generation XK120 with the "old" six-cylinder engine.

So I had just sold the XK120. The money had been in the bank maybe a week. My daughter Stephanie was babysitting for a couple who needed to sell the E-Type to help finance a new business they were starting. I took one look at it and immediately made an offer, which they accepted.

There's a certain look and feel to foreign cars—it's not just the car itself; it's the little chrome pieces, the way the engine is constructed. Every time I look at this car, at the side mirror or the chrome exhaust or the fender, it's like an art object that you drive instead of putting on the wall. It's as interesting today as it was when I bought it in 1987.

I can feel the car running and know exactly what it needs. The engine is so big it has a tendency to overheat in this small, thin-skinned automobile, so when I start the car, I turn on the fuel pump and let it run, and when I hear a different sound in the engine, I know to start it. You have to use little tricks like that.

I do spend a lot of time with the car. I remember one time talking to my wife, Cinda, saying, "When I pass, I'd really like to be buried in the car." She didn't even flinch: "Honey, the car will be sold before your body is cold." She was serious, too.

HILTON HEAD CONCOURS D'ELEGANCE

I first attended the Hilton Head Concours d'Elegance a few years ago, on assignment for a magazine. All the cars were thoughtfully displayed at a golf club on Hilton Head Island, in South Carolina. I've been to bigger and more prestigious car events, but I loved the scale and approachability of this one. There was a great mix of very special cars and, most important, passionate owners. The first day of the event was club day. Car club members lined up in their respective groups on the greens and fairways. There were the expected groups—Porsche, Ferrari, Austin-Healey—but there were some unexpected groups as well, ones I didn't typically see at these kind of shows: 4x4's, Volvos, BMW M1's, and rare, one-off Italian cars. The second day was the Concours: the day all cars were judged in their respective classes and prizes were awarded for the best examples. When I walked around and looked at the plaques that accompanied each car, I was surprised to see that so many of these magical—and often rare—cars came from places nearby: the Carolinas, Georgia, Florida. I had no idea there was such a prolific, passionate, and eclectic classic-car culture in this part of the South. I was inspired not only by the cars but also by the generosity of the owners and the hospitality of the organizers.

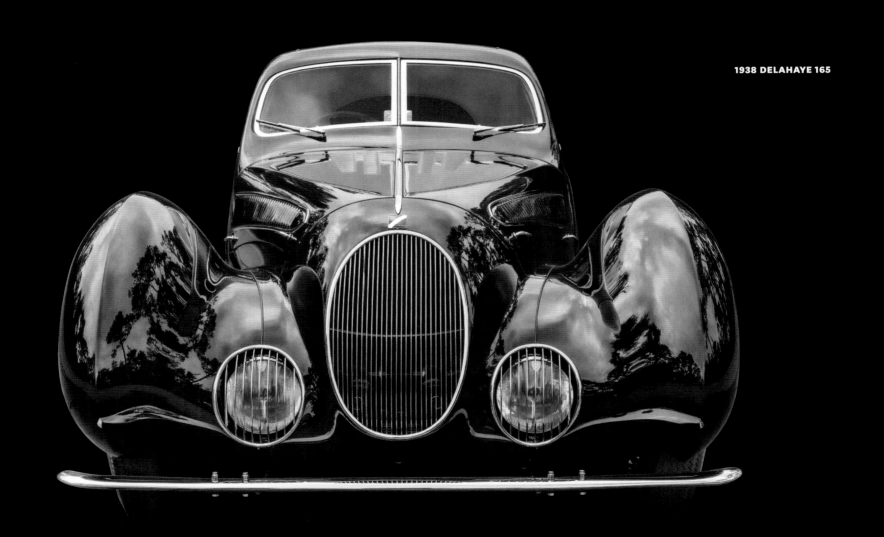

1938 DELAHAYE 165

PETER MULLIN
COLLECTOR & FOUNDER,
MULLIN AUTOMOTIVE MUSEUM

I've been a fan of Delahaye for a long time. It's hard not to fall in love with the soft tapered curves—from the front, the side, the rear. The French, of course, were the best in the world at creating those types of shapes in the prewar era.

The Delahaye 145s and 165s were the outgrowth of the company's attempt to break the world speed record at 200 kph. When they set the new record at Montlhéry, with the 145, and took the record away from the German manufacturers, they then created two 165s, which had a slightly bigger displacement than the 4.5-liter 145s. They thought this car was the perfect combination of sculptural beauty, swoopy curves, and a V12 engine—engineering excellence, performance, and beauty. You look at this car coming down the street, and it doesn't look like it's displacing the air—it looks like it's slicing through the air.

There were only two examples of the 165, built in 1938, one for the Paris Auto Show and one for the New York World's Fair. Ours is the World's Fair car. Acquiring it was a pretty heady experience for me.

It's impossible to look at it without thinking of the beauty that God has created. I was an art major in college, and I've always had an affection for the car's shape and form, as well as its elegance and performance and engineering. Carmakers of that era had that beautiful artistic view. Figoni et Falaschi designed the 165s—they were one of the premier *carrossiers*, or coachbuilders.

The 165s weren't made by a factory; they were made by coachbuilders. You'd buy a chassis, then take it to a *carrossier*, and they would build a shape to envelop the mechanics. They were the artists of the day.

I bought my first Delahaye a little more than forty years ago. I've built up a collection over the years. I've probably got ten, twelve Delahayes. One is probably enough, but if you have a collector's mentality, you end up with more than one because you appreciate what they are. You appreciate that they're works of art, you appreciate that they're special, and you appreciate that there's never going to be anything like them again. They were built before I was born, and they're going to last a lot longer than I am.

I get a huge amount of pleasure out of showing cars, out of driving cars, and out of inviting people to come spend some time celebrating them, looking at the finer aspects of them up close. There shouldn't be some big ring around the cars, warning people to stay away. That's a key part of why we created the Mullin Automotive Museum, to share these spectacular pieces of art with the public, instead of just having them tucked away in a garage somewhere.

1912 HUDSON SPEEDSTER

PAUL IANUARIO
MECHANICAL ENGINEER &
CONCOURS JUDGE

When I was growing up, in the fifties and sixties, parents didn't buy their children cars. They were still trying to buy cars for themselves. If a kid had a car, it was whatever they could afford from doing odd jobs. The car usually needed work. Sometimes it wouldn't even run until you spent some time at the wrecking yard, trying to find parts for it, maybe not even off the same type of car—as long as it fit, that was all you cared about. And all your friends were doing the same thing. Spending time with them, learning things, you developed dexterity. I loved messing with gears. I was a mechanical engineer for more than forty years, and I can trace my career path back to that time.

I gravitate to hundred-year-old cars because that was when automotive engineering was at its purest. There was nothing to copy. You designed and solved problems on your own. If you look at 1910 up to about 1914, that was the golden age, when the saying "Man against the road" actually had meaning.

The first cars were sedans and touring cars, things that were utilitarian. Then car companies realized that some people just wanted to have a car to get out and play on the weekend, go fast, maybe even race against their friends. In 1911 and '12, car companies developed a new body style— some called it a runabout, some called it a speedster, some called it a speed roadster, all different names. They were racing shapes, two bucket seats, no top.

Hudson was a car company that had just been founded in 1909, and they were all about performance. They decided to build a thousand of these cars. It was a performance design named the Mile-a-Minute Speedster—that's 60 mph, which back in 1912 was flying. They shipped the car with a 100 mph speedometer to encourage owners to push the limits of the car. The advertisement for the car actually read, "This car is capable of exceeding its advertised speeds, running boards are removable for all forms of race work and it's particularly competitive in hill climbing."

In 1912, when the standard wage was 25¢ an hour for a ten-hour day—$2.50 a day—any body style of Hudson, including the Speedster, cost $1,600. Needless to say, the goal of producing those thousand Speedsters was never realized. Most historians today estimate that Hudson made fewer than two hundred examples. Mine is number 160.

Most people don't know how to begin working on a hundred-year-old car. The cars are driven off magnetos, which are almost witchcraft, and strange carburetors, strange combustion chambers. If you can understand a car like that, make it function and keep it running well, you're preserving history. That's really what old cars are about.

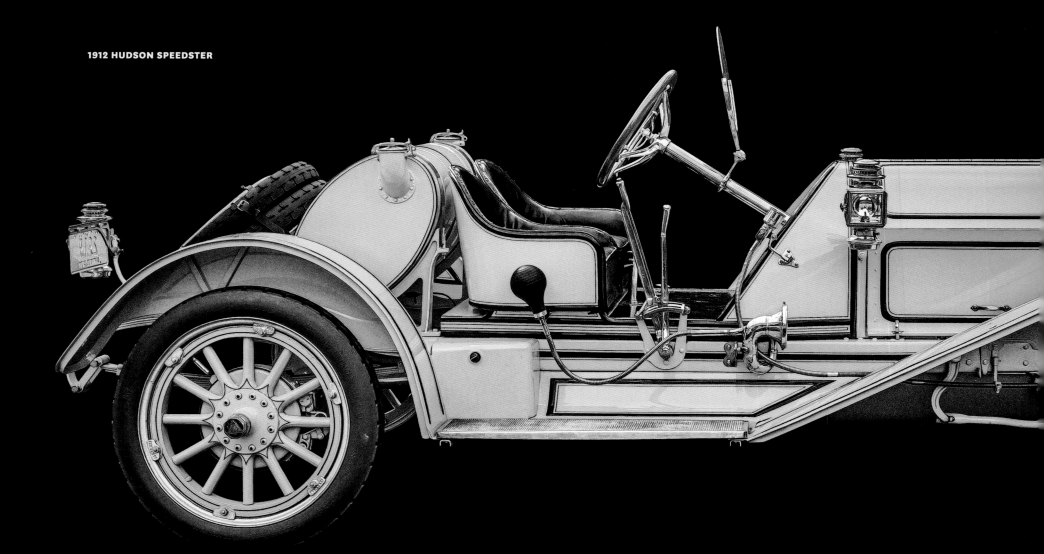

1912 HUDSON SPEEDSTER

"If you can understand a car like that, make it function and keep it running well, you're preserving history. That's really what old cars are about."

—PAUL IANUARIO

1940 AMERICAN BANTAM ROADSTER

**BILL THOMAS
COLLECTOR**

I got interested in Bantams because they were built in my hometown of Butler, Pennsylvania, and my grandfather was one of the early investors in the American Austin company, a predecessor to American Bantam. Austin was a British company until businessmen from Butler convinced them to come to Pennsylvania; the American Austin Car Company was founded in 1929. Of course, that was just when the stock market crashed and the Depression started. By 1934, the company had built about twenty thousand cars—including coupes, pickup trucks, delivery vans, and roadsters—but they couldn't sell enough cars to stay solvent. When the company finally filed for bankruptcy, a gentleman by the name of Roy Evans bought it. He took all the inventory to Florida and sold a lot of the cars down there. Then he reorganized the company as American Bantam and restyled the Austin but still kept it small. That's the reason they called the cars Bantams.

Bantams were advertised as America's first economy car and marketed to consumers as a second car for the household. Most people at the time had a Model A Ford or a Model T or a Packard. But the lady of the house didn't have any way to run errands during the day if her husband drove to work. The Bantam was a car she could drive around town and park easily, because it was so small.

My mother had the American Austin Roadster, the same model I have. As a young boy, I heard stories about her Roadster. The day after the American Austin company went bankrupt, my grandfather also went bankrupt because he owned several thousand shares of stock and lost them all, and so her car was repossessed. She always said that was one of the saddest days in her life. She had stood at her bedroom window and watched them pull it out of the garage. I never saw her in this car. It was gone by the time I was born. I have photos of it, though.

Talking about cars brings back memories. I think that's the big connection for most men. I remember my dad teaching me the basics: how to change a tire, how to set points, and how to replace spark plugs—that kind of thing.

I grew up with fifties and sixties cars—"my vintage." I hope that some of these cars are still around in the future. I go to the Hilton Head Island Cars & Coffee events at the university in Bluffton, and all the kids have muscle cars. That's what they're interested in: the big Dodge Charger with the HEMI, all that stuff.

My intention is to leave these cars to my grandson. He does show some interest in them. I'm hoping that we can keep the cars in the family. My grandson lives in Butler, Pennsylvania, so really, I'll be returning the cars to their birthplace.

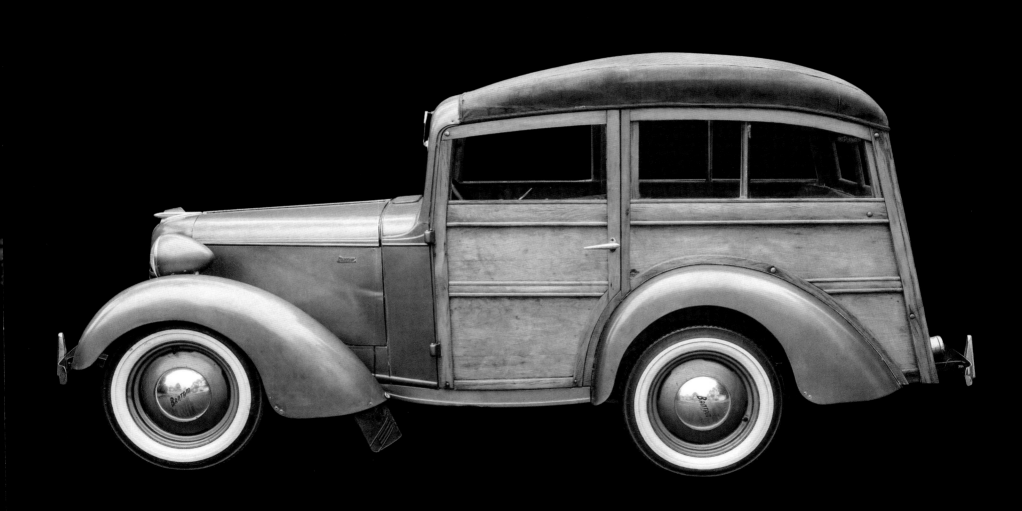

1954 SIATA 8V COUPE

WALTER EISENSTARK
COLLECTOR

In 1957, my father was no longer commuting into New York City; we lived in the suburbs. So he decided to acquire a sports car. That began what turned out to be a two-year hunt. Needless to say, what we passed up between 1957 and 1959 would be a treasure trove of valuable automobiles today. In August 1959, my father decided on a second-production Mercedes Gullwing sold in this country. He had the car for three days, then gave it back to the guy. If you know anything about Gullwing, they're not very nice to drive. About a month later, on September 12, 1959, he bought the Siata. It had nineteen thousand miles on it and, in horse parlance, had been ridden hard and put away wet. It's been in the same family ever since.

Over the next five or six years, it underwent a thorough if amateur mechanical reconstruction, with improvements to make the car viable for grand touring instead of racing. That culminated in '65 with a bare-metal respray by Victor Auto Service in New York. The charge for that at the time was $770.

This car came about from an association Siata had with Fiat. Siata made modification parts, but in 1949, after World War II, they started building cars, all of which had some form of Fiat power. Around the same time, Fiat decided they needed to build a car for their executives so they wouldn't be driving Alfas or Lancias or Ferraris. They designed an engine and a chassis and

suspension, and acquired fifty-five engines and fifty-five suspension pieces, though all fifty-five Siatas used a unique Siata engine—two four-cylinder engines put on a common block to form a V-shaped engine. At the time, Fiat believed that Ford owned the rights to the term "V8," so the engine itself and all the cars it went into are known as "Otto Vu"—8V.

The coupes, which total eighteen, were built by two different coachbuilders and have five-speed gearboxes, whereas the Fiats had only four-speed gearboxes.

This car is the next-to-last one built. It was built in '53, came to New York in '53, and was licensed in '54. Before we bought it in 1959, it had three prior owners, all of whom raced it. After the bare-metal respray in '65 and a new interior, it spent the next fifty-two years in tours, some hill climbs, and a lot of automobile shows. It was all over the country.

There are a hell of a lot of really great old cars, once you look beyond Ferrari or Cadillac or Alfa Romeo. The obvious ones. If you have a Ferrari—and I do—everyone automatically thinks you're rich, even though that's not necessarily the case. But the guy who owns a Fiat Otto Vu, or the guy who owns a Lagonda that was built in the thirties, or the guy who owns a Cisitalia or a Voisin—these guys really have *cars*, as well as a depth of knowledge of automobiles that exist beyond what's popular.

1982 PORSCHE 928

DALE MOSS
CAR DETAILER

I was a fourth generation in the supermarket business—ours was independent, privately owned, not associated with any chain. I grew up close to Pittsburgh, and my dad and I shared a passion for cars. He was twenty years older than my mother and had Marmons and Packards and all these wonderful cars. My first car was a 1957 Corvette.

A race car driver by the name of Don Yenko, a pretty famous guy in Western Pennsylvania who owned Yenko Chevrolet, did autocrossing in supermarket parking lots on Sundays. There were blue laws in the area—if you had more than six employees, your business had to be closed on Sundays—so we would set up courses in supermarket parking lots all over Western Pennsylvania. These short courses were laid out with decreasing-radius and S turns, and we'd try to set the fastest time. This was in the late fifties. It was accepted at the time—the local police were fine with it, and so was my dad because he was a car guy.

In the seventies, I became familiar with the design and handling of German cars. My wife and I each had an Audi 5000; I've owned a lot of BMWs. The Porsche was a natural move, especially for the handling and steering. I bought this 928 in 1982 at a Porsche-Audi dealership outside of Pittsburgh.

The 928 was the first clean-sheet Porsche built without any Volkswagen parts. Porsche designed the car in 1977, but production ended by 1995 because the 911 purists, the rear-engine guys, never accepted it. They wanted a pure sports car, but the 928 is really a grand touring car that Porsche hoped would compete with the Mercedes SL.

Porsche made a big deal out of the rear axle in this car, what they call the Weissach axle. But it wasn't the only Porsche that had it. Typically, with an independent rear suspension, when you come out of the throttle during deceleration, the tires go to a positive camber rather than negative; with the Weissach axle, however, the wheels kick out to a negative camber when you come off the throttle, so you go through a turn on rails. It's like it doesn't move.

This car has lived a very sheltered life. It's always been in heated and air-conditioned facilities. It's been in the rain very occasionally, but it's never seen snow or ice.

In 1994, I built a home on Hilton Head Island, South Carolina, and my ambition was to be still driving this car when I turned seventy. I've not only accomplished that goal, I've exceeded it by six years.

1953 ARDEX THREE-WHEELER

JEFF LANE
FOUNDER, LANE MOTOR MUSEUM

Ardex was a French company that in the thirties made tiny three-wheelers, kind of like a Morgan three-wheeler. But after World War II, when Europe was decimated, people only walked or rode bicycles, so Ardex went to a more "austere" car—microcars. This model is made of plywood, with bicycle wheels and a 50cc motor. Very spartan. But on a rainy or cold day, instead of riding a scooter, you could be riding inside a microcar. *Luxurious* is an odd word for them, but they were. They also had to be very cheap. They had to cost just a bit more than a high-end bicycle.

This one's been restored, but it's fairly original to what came out of that period. We can't figure out exactly how many they made, but this one was toward the end of the car's lifetime.

They were gone by around 1955. That's when what you'd call a proper small car came out, something like a mini, and it wiped out all the microcar makers.

1975 PINZGAUER 710M

TODD CRUTCHLEY
FINANCIAL ADVISER

I was in Hawaii, and one of those adventure companies was picking up everyone in one of these, and I thought, *That's pretty cool.*

Vintage trucks were a new thing for me. The last owner of this truck was the Swiss army, which was about to replace it with a new generation of vehicles.

I drive it about every two weeks. I'll take it up on a mud run, then drive it straight to a car show. Ten years ago, when there wasn't as much development, I had more places to play. I don't have any hills by me—you go up into the mountains for that—but I'd go running in the mud in the marsh.

People enjoy seeing the car. As I drive by, I get a lot of thumbs-ups and waves. My uncle collected old cars, and he had a term for a vehicle like this—he would call it a "wonderful nuisance." Because everywhere you go, everyone's stopping you, asking about it, and then they want to tell you the story of their car, something they loved or had some affection toward. So you stop and you share. It's a human experience. I enjoy it.

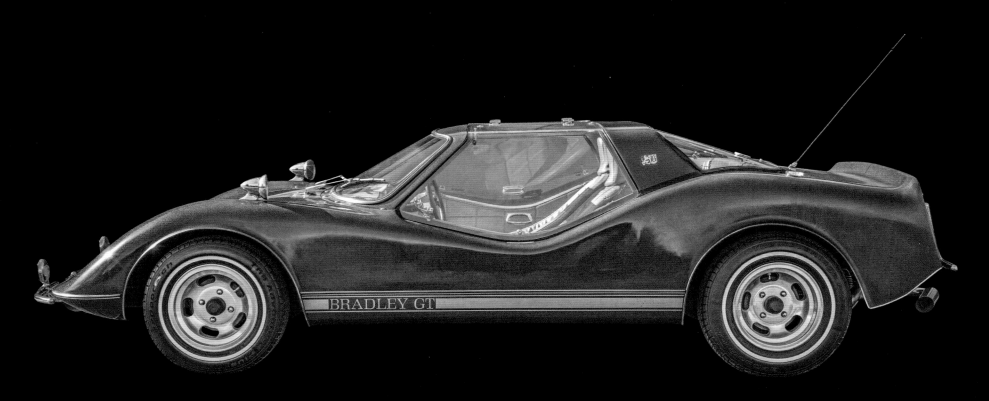

JEFF DUNHAM

COMEDIAN & VENTRILOQUIST

——✠——

PERSONAL COLLECTION

When I was five years old, I had a big collection of Hot Wheels—so I knew what was cool, what I loved. It wasn't until junior high that I started paying attention to real cars.

One day when I was thirteen, I opened up *Popular Mechanics* and saw an ad for a Bradley GT, a kit car built on a Volkswagen platform. I had never heard of a kit car, but I was building digital watches, building and flying kit helicopters, and I thought it was the coolest thing that you could build a car yourself. I wrote a letter to the Bradley GT company saying I'd be their local representative in Dallas, and all they had to do was send me the kit for free. Somehow, I figured I'd find a Volkswagen and then be able to do it. But I never got the kit.

Fast-forward to 1994. I see a Dodge Viper in a showroom window. I think, *Finally, somebody my age who had Hot Wheels as a kid is turning them into real cars.* It's a legitimate production—vehicles that looked like a Hot Wheels—and I thought that was so cool. I bought a Viper, owned it for a few years, and had a blast driving it.

The real car collecting didn't happen until later, about ten years ago. I don't go on expensive trips. I don't care about fancy clothes. But I got that car bug.

It got pretty aggressive, but I think I'm fairly smart about it. I have three rules: One, I have to have a good chance of at least breaking even when I eventually sell the cars or, better, of coming out ahead; I'm not going to buy something that's going to depreciate 30 percent as soon as I drive it off the line. Two, the cars have to be used—they can't be trophies. Finally, these cars have to be interesting to me and start conversations. They have to have a soul.

When I was in high school, there was a guy named Carl Wescott who was the big local car salesman. He'd get on television with what he pretended were live commercials—"How're you doing this Saturday night? We're here at the dealership. Here are the cars we have right now."—walking down the line, all the prices in big numbers on the windshields. I already had ventriloquist dummies and knew that comedy was what I was going to do forever. I was already doing shows. I thought, *I can do those commercials.* I kept calling his office obsessively. Finally, I got in. I gave him my pitch, and he said, "I've got a small Datsun dealership in Richardson. I'll have you do those commercials."

For four years, I did commercials for Courtesy Pontiac & Datsun and learned all about Datsuns. Every six thousand miles, I got a new 280ZX demo car. And I got paid on top of it. When all that came to an end, I knew I could get a heck of a deal on a Datsun, so I bought a 280ZX. I went everywhere in that car.

My first real career break came in 1990 when I was on *The Tonight Show* with Johnny Carson. And I bought my next car, the 1990 Nissan 300ZX. Got a personalized plate that said TEXAS DUMMY.

I parked the 280ZX in Dallas, out by my parents' garage with a tarp over it. Every six months, my dad put a new tarp over it because the Texas weather beat the cover to hell. It sat there for twenty-two years. I never wanted to get rid of it because it was the first big thing the dummies had paid for. I always had a plan that if I made enough money, I would bring that car to LA and refurbish it. And that's exactly what happened. The motor was fine, too.

The Hard Hat Hauler and the Calico Surfer were both brought to life by designer George Barris. His creations were rolling entertainment. These are full-sized, drivable "Odd Rods"! He was thinking like a twelve-year-old kid when he made them, and that's why I appreciate them so much.

Barris didn't design the Hard Hat Hauler, but he was crazy enough to take an existing plastic model and build it *for real*. It's half forklift–half hot rod, has a stack of blowers 3 feet tall sitting on top of a giant engine, and wears an enormous polished hard hat. How is this an actual vehicle that runs and drives? It's not easy, but it does!

The Calico Surfer is more of an actual car. You can drive it somewhat comfortably. It's still an insane piece of artwork that only someone like Barris could dream up and bring to life. It's an awesome piece of American automotive history that could only come out of the '60s. More important, it starts a fun conversation with anyone who sees it.

And those Bradley kit cars? A few years ago, I started looking online, and sure enough, there were a handful of them for sale. They were so cheap—three thousand bucks for a car—and it's a Volkswagen. It's a piece of crap, but to me, it still looked so cool. And yet I kept thinking, *How can I have a car collection and not get the car that started it all for me?* Besides, it's the most successful kit car in history.

I talked to this friend of mine about the Bradley. He looked at me like I was crazy. All he saw was something pretending to be a fancy sports car.

The kid in me was like, *So?* As kids, we put on costumes even though it doesn't actually make us superheroes.

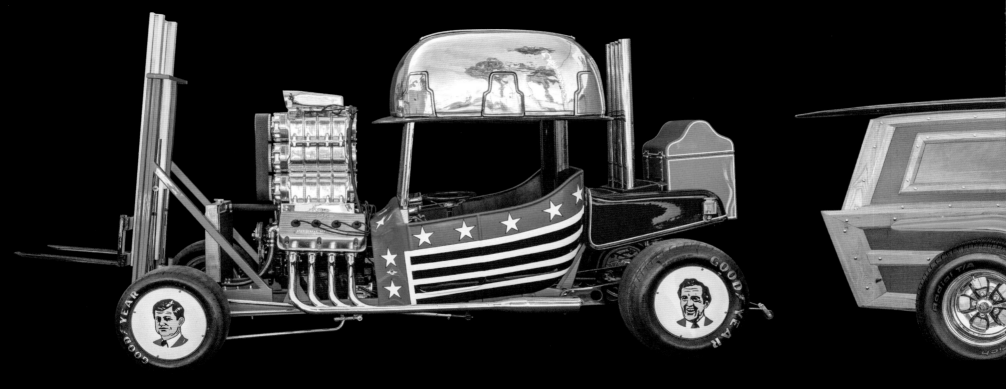

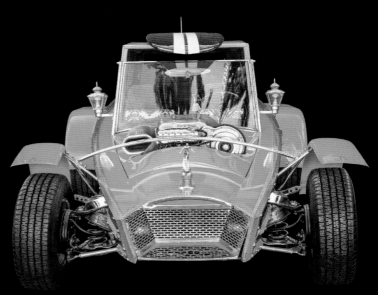

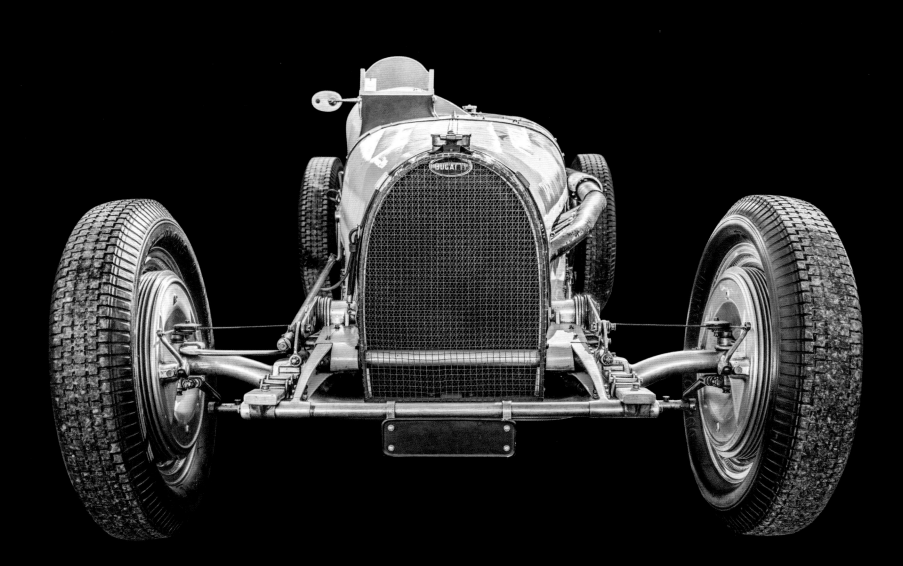

MARC NEWSON

INDUSTRIAL DESIGNER

———— ‖ ————

1933 BUGATTI TYPE 59

The two things I was obsessed with as a kid were cars and wristwatches. I was incredibly mechanically minded. My grandfather had a small workshop, and I'd go in there and tinker with things. When my uncle gave me my first wristwatch, the first thing I did—to his horror—was take it to pieces, and then try to build a new case for it out of Plexiglas. I think I was nine or something. I just loved the idea that a watch or a car was its own little universe.

I've only ever loved old cars, both as a means of transport and also as objects in themselves. I grew up in Australia, and, as in most of the United States, you simply can't live without a car. They're very much part of the culture. There used to be big car production in Australia. General Motors had the Holden, which was a generic vehicle designed and produced in Australia. Ford had the Falcon, which was the alternative to the Holden.

Up until recently, Australia was a little bit like Cuba in a way, in that people would cherish their old foreign cars and keep them running for a very long time, because import taxes for cars were prohibitive, at least when I was growing up there. There were a lot of exotic cars. A lot of people out in the rural parts of Australia owned Citroëns because their suspension went up and down and, contrary to popular opinion, they were reliable. If you were wealthy, you'd have a Rolls-Royce, because they were the most reliable—the engines would last millions of miles.

The 1933 Bugatti Type 59 was anomalous for me—I wasn't interested in any other cars from the era. I never would have imagined in my wildest dreams that I would know how to find one, let alone have one. It was not only a thing of beauty; it was just so exotic and preposterous and improbable.

This one somehow just fell into my lap, really. It belonged to an elderly collector who had arguably one of the greatest collections of Bugattis that's ever existed. I've been informed that this is the best of the 59s. It has been incredibly well maintained and is highly patinated, with all the signs of age in the right ways but not tatty. And it's never been in a serious accident—for a Grand Prix car, that's extremely rare. People drove these things like there was no tomorrow. Its body is original, as is every single one of its mechanical components, every little thing.

These cars are quirky and sometimes unreliable, though I find they're not as unreliable as people like to make out. They're almost like living

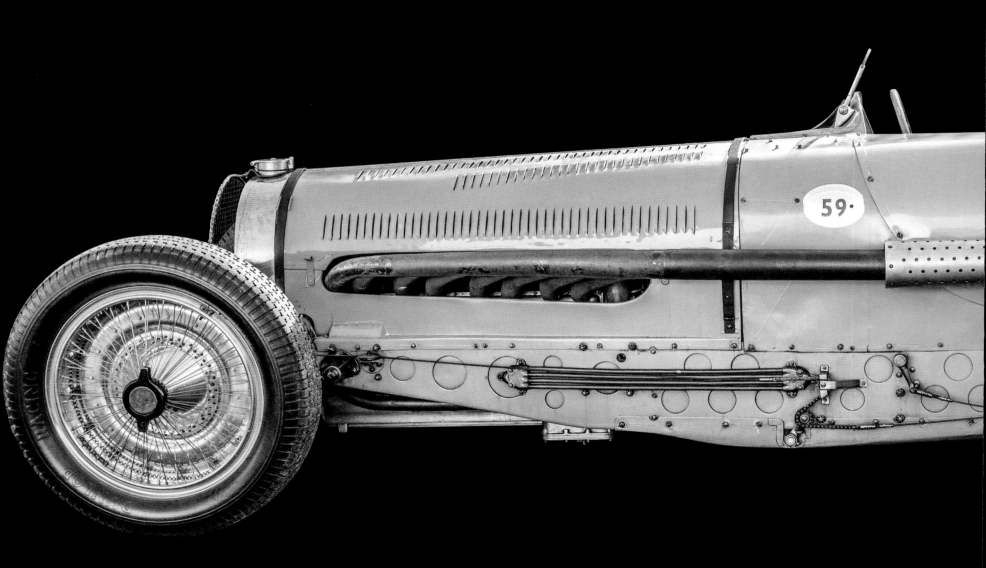

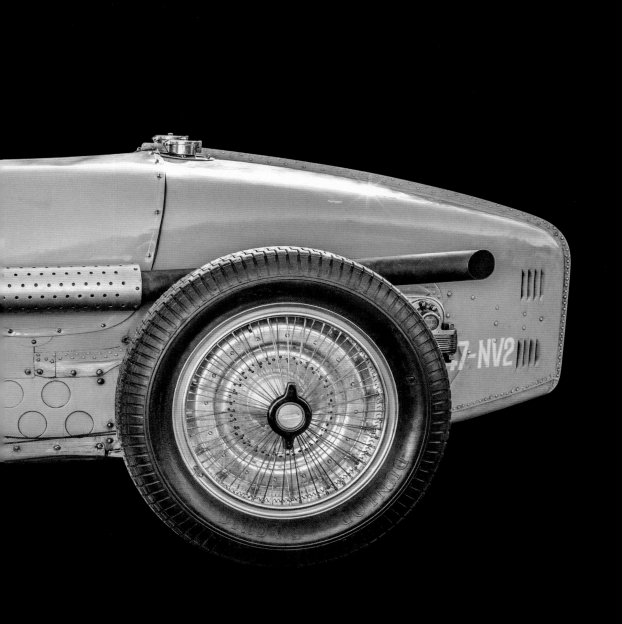

things, with a whole multitude of organs and moving parts, and when all is working well, when you're driving along at what feels like 150 mph but is actually about 60, it's just brilliant.

I took this Type 59 to the Mille Miglia, and I've got to say, it performed flawlessly. I don't think the poor thing had ever done more than a hundred miles in a single stretch in its whole life; I did probably twelve hundred miles in three days. My wife did it with me. She's done the Mille with me a couple different times in different cars, and she claims to this day that this one was the most enjoyable ride—the most fun and the most comfortable. She literally fell asleep. I just can't fathom how you fall asleep in that car during an open-road endurance race, but she did. Go figure.

ROMAN GRUDININ

PARTS BUSINESS DEVELOPMENT ANALYST, VOLVO

———— H ————

1982 LADA 1300/VAZ 2103

Go back in time to the Soviet Union of the 1950s, following World War II. The country was disheveled after being bombarded by the German army. The country's industry had been completely focused on making war equipment, but once the war was over, they needed to start a car industry. Unlike the United States, which already had an advanced car industry in the fifties, the Soviet Union was essentially starting from scratch.

First, the country partnered with Ford, which helped build a plant in Russia that made an American-style car. But that plant was soon too small for demand. Come the mid-sixties, over twenty years since the war had ended, they were expanding the economy, so more people would need cars.

In 1958, they made a car called ZAZ. It was crappy, but it was a quick fix to make cars accessible to many, many more people. It was a two-door, four-passenger, rear-engine car very similar to the Fiat 600, 27 horsepower.

Soviet premier Nikita Khrushchev loved all things small and economically friendly, but when he was on his way out of office, the government decided they needed a bigger car. They weren't going to work with the Germans because they

had been at war with them, so they said no to Volkswagen. Peugeots were too weak for Russian conditions. The Fiats were also weak, but the Russians partnered with them because the owner of Fiat had a financial interest in the Communist Party of Italy, and the Soviet Union liked that.

They bought six Fiat 124 cars and shipped them to the Soviet Union for testing. The cars all fell apart in the first thousand kilometers. So they started coming up with engineering fixes for the issues. They made around eight hundred changes. Thicker metal, bulkier suspension and drivetrain. The car was tailored to the Russian winters. It had a hand-starter so you could fire it up with a dead battery, and you could drain coolant from the engine block so you could leave the car outside overnight in Siberia. They didn't make their own tires or glass, or components like the starter or distributor, but the full body, engine, transmission, drivetrain, axles, and brake drums were all made at the plant. The car was completely different and basically unkillable. Just the shape of the Fiat was left.

In 1970, the first car rolls off the assembly line. In '71, the first wagon. In '72, the VAZ-2103, a luxury version of the sedan. This is my car. They made it from '72 to '84 without significant changes. In the USSR, the car was officially called a VAZ 2103. Outside the USSR, this car would be called a LADA 1300.

I grew up spending about half my time in Ukraine while my parents settled in the United States. I associate Ladas with my childhood. They were very common in Ukraine, because after the collapse of the Soviet Union in the mid-nineties, there were a lot of cars left over. Ladas were taxis when I was growing up in Ukraine. My friends and family had them. I remember the sounds and the smells of those cars. Then all of a sudden, time passes and they disappear. If you go to Ukraine now, you'll still see some Ladas here and there, but it's like seeing a Buick from the seventies on the street today in the United States—it's rare.

However, this particular car was a luxury model. And in those days, Ladas were extremely expensive in the Soviet Union. At the time, the average doctor made about 200 rubles per month. This car was 8,000 rubles, and my particular model was 8,700 rubles, no financing available. Even if you had the cash, there was still a waiting list of five to seven years. Then one day you get a postcard in the mail saying, "You have three days to bring your cash to this address and pick up your vehicle. You can pick the model but not the color." Getting a car was very tough. Cars were real status symbols.

You could also win this type of car in the Soviet lottery system—they would donate models with minor defects, like scratches, because it was less expensive than going back and fixing them. When I bought the car, the woman who sold it to me told me a story about winning it in the lottery, which I didn't believe at the time. A year and a half later, she called my grandmother and said, "I have this paper from the lottery—do you want it? Otherwise I'm going to throw it out." Everything she'd said was right there, detailed on a 1982 document, with her same address from when I purchased the car from her. She was the first owner. She paid one ruble for that car in the lottery. I'm the second owner.

I have Soviet tires on the car. It's really special to consider that those tires drove on the land of a country that doesn't exist anymore. The people assembling the car during the Cold War had no idea it would eventually wind up in so-called enemy territory in a garage with mats under the tires and a painted floor. Owning this Lada is my way of preserving the history I grew up with. It's like a history lesson on wheels.

CHRIS MITCHELL

MEDIA EXECUTIVE

——— H ———

1965 JEEP CJ TUXEDO PARK

When I was a college kid, the girl I was dating had a family summerhouse in Michigan, where I spent a couple of summers working on the lake. Her grandfather had a red 1965 Jeep, with the same three-on-the-tree as mine. It was the most fun thing to drive ever. We'd go to the drive-in theater and put a blanket on the hood with the windshield down.

Then, many years later, I saw this one for sale and had to have it. Now it's my beach runner. Driving around East Hampton, New York, is a lot like what I was doing twenty-five, thirty years ago in Northern Michigan: little country back roads and beach lanes.

There's no status in owning one of these. It doesn't want to go more than 40 mph. Everyone wants a Land Rover, but there's something really honest and American and modest about this little Jeep. It's not there to impress anybody, which is what's great about it.

Buying one will never be a smart decision on paper, because it doesn't have the safety standards. But nothing beats the experience of being in a car with no top and no doors, running down a beach lane in the summertime.

JONATHAN EINHORN

LAWYER

—— ¦¦ ——

1965 AUSTIN-HEALEY 3000 MK III

I bought this 1965 Austin-Healey 3000 Mark III in '79 through something called *Bargain News*, a regional newspaper, that had cars for sale.

I had the same model in college, a '65—but that one was yellow and black. I bought it in 1967, I think, and it took me everywhere. Rain, snow, shine. I was in western Massachusetts, which was pretty snowy. The car was great. It never failed me.

I got married in 1971. My first wife decided, rightly, that it was not a great family car. I got rid of it in 1973 and bought a Volvo.

As soon as I could, I bought this car. I owned it until about five or six years ago. I wasn't driving it much, really; it sat in the garage. I needed money to pay taxes, so I put an ad on eBay and sold it to a doctor from Newport News, Virginia. He came up with a U-Haul trailer, and I thought I'd never see the car again.

One day my son Jeffrey says, "Pop, I'm doing a car show in Prospect Park in Brooklyn. Can you come down?" So I said sure, I'd come down. When I got there, I parked, looked across the lot, and spotted the Austin-Healey. I knew immediately it was the car. I've never seen another Healey with that stripe, and the louvered hood.

I walked toward it and said to Jeff, "I wonder if the doctor is here. I'd sure like to talk to him about the car." He said, "Well, Pop, take a look at the license plate." I looked toward the back—there was a New York plate. He said, "I bought it from the doctor."

It was a total surprise. He had bought it maybe two or three months earlier and just kept it in New York, didn't tell me about it.

I have a strong emotional connection to this car. This is the car I used to drive up to the Berkshires in to visit the kids at camp. This is the car my boys borrowed when they had a new girlfriend. This is the car they took to the prom, or whenever they were trying to impress somebody.

And it feels kind of neat having it back, actually. It's probably the only car I've ever driven where I can't help but smile when I drive it. It is a member of the family, forever.

IVAN DUTTON

CAR RESTORATION SPECIALIST

——— || ———

1952 SALMSON

This is a 1952 Salmson, which is a French car. My love for Salmsons started in 1950, after the war, when my dad bought a 1926 Salmson Grand Prix for fifty-two pounds, ten pence. I helped him work on it—it was the first car that I ever worked on, actually. It was a bit of a wreck.

My dad used to take me to school in it, and all the kids used to laugh. They'd say, "What's that funny old car?" and "How fast does it go?" And I'd say it could do 85 mph. And the kids said, "My dad's car does faster than that." Yeah, well, not in 1926 it didn't! If you get taken to school in a vintage car now, kids will say, "Well, that family's got a few quid."

Before the war, my dad raced with a chap called George Newman, who was the importer for Salmsons in England. They used to race at Brooklands, and they won their class in the 200-mile race. But in 1926, my dad was just a mechanic—he could have never afforded to buy a Salmson then. It would be like buying a Lamborghini.

My dad actually went and worked at the Salmson factory, in Billancourt, just outside Paris. So he spoke really good French, which was surprising for an ordinary man from the Peabody estates. His number at the factory was eight, and every time he'd see a Salmson, he'd go looking for his number eight stamped somewhere.

Years later, I got into Salmsons myself: read about them, started collecting bits for a special build. I was looking through my dad's old correspondence and found a letter from George Newman. Apparently, my dad had written to George and asked to buy his old car, and George had written back saying, "No, but when I do sell it, I'll keep you in mind." And I thought, *Well, we've got to have a Salmson, really.* I found my first one in Portugal.

I always wanted to be a racing driver, but lack of education held me back a bit there. I was terrible at school. But I knew all about cars. I was fabulous at metalwork. When I left school, I couldn't get a job, which turned out to be good, really, because I had to work for myself. I opened a car business, and when I was about thirty-two, my nephew helped me get a fabulous sponsor, and I went racing. I won the Peter Collins Allcomers Trophy for the most outstanding newcomer to motor racing because I won eighteen races, in a Ford Escort, straight off. Nobody could believe it. It was purely by chance. I wonder sometimes how it happened, and I realized that it's because I spent my whole life thinking of nothing else.

HENRY FORD MUSEUM ARCHIVE

The impact that Ford had on Americans—and everyone else—cannot be underestimated. Ford not only changed the automobile industry; it changed the world.

The company's archive has so many cool cars, from the early incarnations to the iconic one-off creations to the Mustangs and the Lincoln Presidential Limousines. The Presidential Limousines, as a group, are amazing, especially when considering how they evolved stylistically—from big, luxurious curves to wedge shapes and clean lines. Those cars are not just examples of how industrial automobile design progressed but also such a cool way to contextualize our national history.

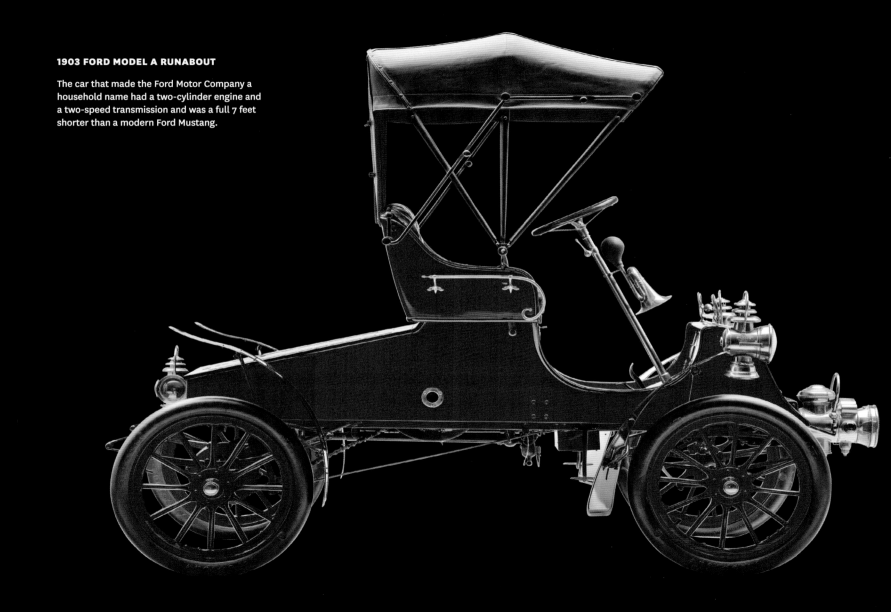

1903 FORD MODEL A RUNABOUT

The car that made the Ford Motor Company a household name had a two-cylinder engine and a two-speed transmission and was a full 7 feet shorter than a modern Ford Mustang.

1908 FORD MODEL S ROADSTER

The Model S was basically a Model N, a hot-selling car at the time with a 15-hp inline-four engine, but with running boards popularized by the Model R.

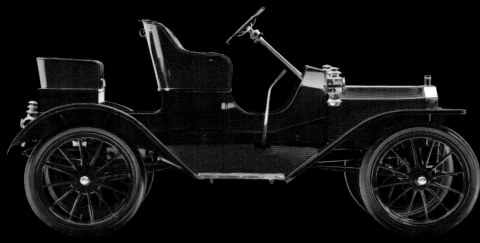

1914 FORD MODEL T TOURING CAR

Henry Ford gave a number of Model T cars to his friend the naturalist John Burroughs, including this one, which was produced the same year Ford fully implemented his moving assembly line at the company's plant in Highland Park, Michigan.

1941 LINCOLN CONTINENTAL CONVERTIBLE— EDSEL FORD *(OPPOSITE, ABOVE)*

While the Lincoln Continental was an instant hit as a production vehicle beginning in 1940, the model started its life as this custom car created by Edsel Ford, with help from Lincoln designers, after a trip to Europe in 1938.

1965 FORD MUSTANG CONVERTIBLE, SERIAL NUMBER 1 *(OPPOSITE, BELOW)*

This is the first Ford Mustang ever produced at the Rouge plant in Dearborn, Michigan, in 1964. Back then, that meant a 164-horsepower V-8, a three-speed automatic transmission, and a sticker price of $3,334.

1939 LINCOLN PRESIDENTIAL LIMOUSINE, USED BY FRANKLIN DELANO ROOSEVELT *(BELOW)*

The very first limo purpose-built for presidential use, this 1939 Lincoln was known as the "Sunshine Special" because Franklin D. Roosevelt used to love riding in it with the convertible top down. It was retrofitted with armor and bullet-resistant tires after the attack on Pearl Harbor in 1941.

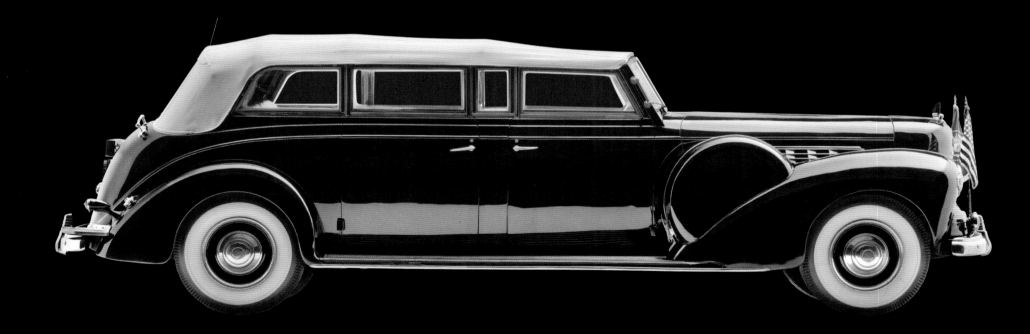

1950 LINCOLN PRESIDENTIAL LIMOUSINE, USED BY DWIGHT D. EISENHOWER *(BELOW)*

Originally built for President Harry S. Truman, this 21-foot-long, 6,500-pound limo also saw use by Presidents Eisenhower, Kennedy, and Johnson. It was Eisenhower who added the distinctive plastic "bubble" top.

1961 LINCOLN CONTINENTAL PRESIDENTIAL LIMOUSINE, USED BY JOHN F. KENNEDY *(OPPOSITE, ABOVE)*

This is probably the most famous limousine in the world: the convertible in which, on November 22, 1963, President John F. Kennedy was assassinated. Amazingly, the limo stayed in use until 1977, though it was rebuilt with titanium armor plating and a permanent roof, and repainted from midnight blue to black.

1972 LINCOLN CONTINENTAL PRESIDENTIAL LIMOUSINE, USED BY RONALD REAGAN *(OPPOSITE, BELOW)*

This 10,440-pound armored tank was used by Presidents Richard Nixon, Gerald Ford, Jimmy Carter, Ronald Reagan, and George H. W. Bush. When Reagan was shot by John Hinckley Jr. in March 1981, this car carried him to the hospital.

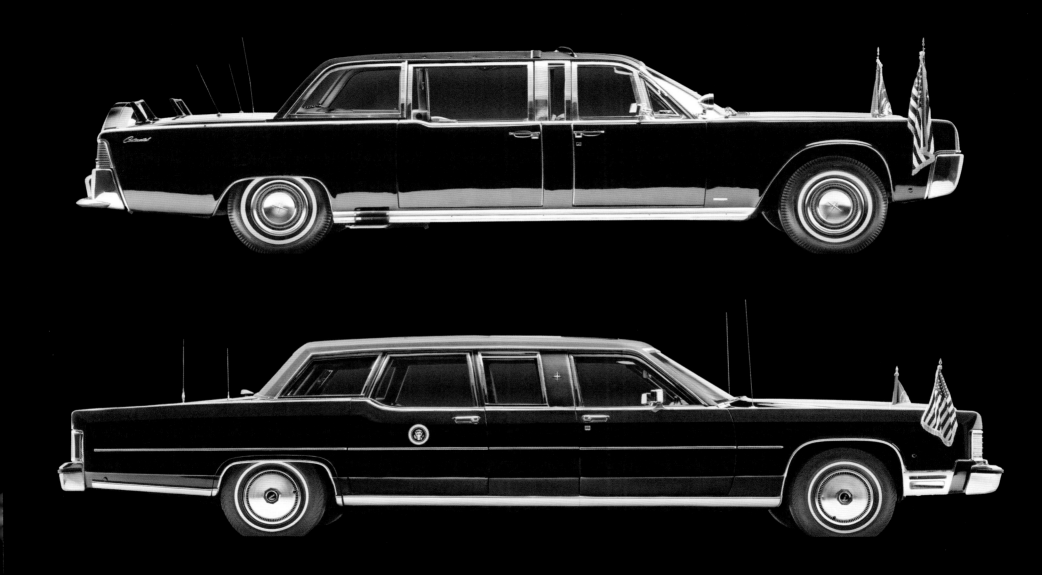

JOE RICHARDSON

FOUNDER, THE BEAUTIFUL NOISE

—— H ——

1967 BMW 2000C

I think I bonded with cars almost before I bonded with people. Nobody in my family is in the car business or anything like that, but I remember as a kid in England, on the motorway, having this uncanny ability to know a car immediately. I'd say, "There goes a Rolls-Royce Silver Shadow," or "There goes a Mini Cooper" or whatever it was. I'm talking about from three, four years old. I thought of all the cars as my friends. I was a lonely little kid, anyway.

What got me about this BMW was, it was a car I didn't know existed. I found it by accident in a shop in Santa Monica. The owners weren't even going to sell it; they were just holding it for a friend. The cool thing about the 2000C is that from the back, it looks like any other seventies BMW coupe, but from the front, you get the glass, the fog lamps, and all that stuff.

I know cars inside and out, so discovering a new car was almost unheard-of for me. Except I realized that I kind of did know the car. Back in England, when I was young, my parents had an old BMW 1800, the four-door version of this car. In the early seventies, we used to take the car to Portugal in the summertime for picnics. It had no air-conditioning, and I remember so clearly what that car smelled like on a hot day.

I wasn't in the market for a car, or even in the mood, but it was so perfect and so unusual. I thought, *If the trunk smells like I remember . . .* I opened the trunk—exact same smell. Suddenly all these old memories from that time in my life came flooding back.

I've had faster cars, more expensive cars, cars that were more admired in collector circles, but there's just something about this little BMW. There's no way to be in a rush in this car. It makes a lovely sound, but like a friend of mine says, it couldn't peel the skin off a cold cup of coffee. It will probably do 100 mph if you've got the time and the nerve, but I wouldn't want to panic-stop this car from a speed above, say, 30 or 40 mph. It might not end well.

I think people now want things that are much more obvious and immediate. Whereas this car has a manual shifter, it doesn't have power steering, it doesn't have air-conditioning, it's not incredibly fast, so you're conscious of the situations you're putting the car into. You can't be casual or laissez-faire about the way you drive it. It makes you very focused on the actual experience of driving, of navigating, of listening to the car.

MAGNUS WALKER

PORSCHE COLLECTOR & CUSTOMIZER

——————— ++ ———————

1971 PORSCHE 911T

Growing up as a kid in working-class England, I didn't have any fancy cars in my household. My father was a salesman, and he had company cars. When I was ten years old, England ruled the world arena of motorsports—in 1976, James Hunt was Formula One world champion and Barry Sheene was world motorcycle champion. I watched a lot of motorsports with my dad as a kid. That's where my love affair with cars began.

This is the second Porsche I ever bought. It's a 1971 911T, a car I refer to as Car Number 277.

I bought it at the Pomona Swap Meet here in California in 1999. The car had already been modified, in the sense that it had a 2.7-liter motor in it instead of the 2.2-liter motor that would have initially been in the car. The first thing I did was make it resemble a 1973 Carrera RS, which is one of the most iconic Porsches of that era, by adding real RS flares and a Carrera ducktail. Then I joined the Porsche Owner Club in 2002 and went down what I call the Porsche Slippery Slope of modifying for performance.

That's one of the greatest things about Porsches—they're easy to modify. You can make them go faster, handle better, stop better.

For a six-year period, I did forty, fifty track days a year in Car 277. I've driven that car to Laguna Seca and back a dozen times. I've raced it at Thunderhill California Speedway, Las Vegas Motor Speedway, Phoenix Raceway. I've raced it at VIR. It's what I call a streetable track car, a sport purpose build, meaning it's not a fully dedicated race car in the sense that it's completely stripped and roll caged, but it has all the necessary performance upgrades—fire system, roll bar, safety harness—to actually do track days and still have spirited fun on the street.

What I love about Car 277 is that it's never been fully restored. It's always been modified for a purpose: to go faster or stop better or handle better. Judged by the sum of its parts, it's nothing special. It didn't race anywhere fancy like Le Mans or Daytona or Sebring. It was built on a budget when I had the funds to work on it. As my driving skill level progressed, so did the car, but I always kept it at a place where I could drive it to the racetrack and back, or wherever I wanted on the street. It's never had a big motor in it. I can keep my foot planted because it doesn't have a ton of horsepower. The greatest thing about the 277 is that it's a car that was built to be driven.

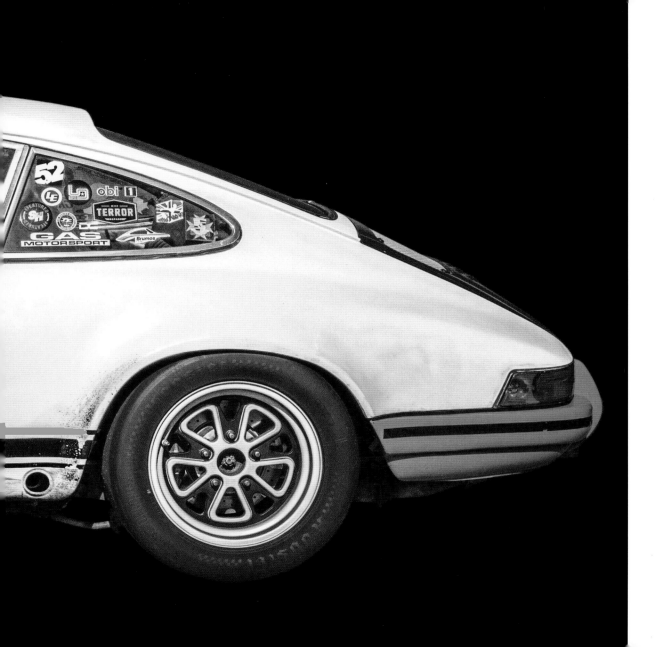

Nothing beats driving in an early air-cooled Porsche, because it engages all the five senses. It's visceral, exciting—the speed's deceptive in those cars. It feels like you're going faster than you are, compared with a new car in which you're going 120 mph and it feels like 80. In an old car, going 80 feels like 120.

With Porsche, my collection is all about variety. It's not just the 911s—it's the 924s, 928s, 944s, 968s, 914s. As long as there's a Porsche crest on the hood, it's a Porsche. It doesn't have to be a 911. It's a journey, and no two drives are the same.

I just collect what I like. It's not based on price. It's based purely on what I want to own and what I want to drive. Maybe it's a little bit of thinking outside the box, but I go by my gut feeling. It either feels right to me or it doesn't.

I've had Car 277 for nearly twenty years, longer than any other car. It's in my DNA. I call it my favorite pair of old jeans: it just fits, and I feel comfortable in it.

NATE HRANEK

DESIGNER, TESLA

—— H ——

1965 CHEVROLET MALIBU

My first encounter with classic American cars was with my uncle Junie in his garage. I would hang out there from time to time and watch him work. He had a 1961 red Chevy Impala. His son Anthony had a Chevelle. My dad had a Chevy truck. You were either a Chevy guy or a Ford guy. They were Chevy guys. But I had no idea that I would go into cars at that point.

I always liked to build. In design school, I went through the sketching process as quickly as I could so I could start building whatever was on the paper. I started in special effects for movies and television in LA. As "special effects" moved into "special effects vehicles," the *vehicle* part took off for me. That led me to work for a company that designed vehicles for movies, and then in the design studio of General Motors.

So I'm working at GM with a bunch of motorheads. Many of the guys had older cars, a lot of Novas, and I was trying to decide what I wanted. And then my wife, Jen, became pregnant with our first child, Vance, and the search got serious. I've heard all the stories: *I wish I did this; I wish I did that.* I knew I had to figure this out before I had a kid.

That's when I found this car in San Diego. I remember going down there and picking it up.

I didn't really know much about it. It was typical Chevy blue, and I liked its clean lines, kind of like a square when you look at it from the side—that clean side profile. I had to have it. I knew it was going to be a long, slow process to restore it, but it would be manageable. Getting it was the hurdle.

So I had the car I liked. Being in the industry, my first thought was, *It's time to start making it my own*, but I didn't want to make it too crazy custom. I put in the 350 V8 engine, and made some other subtle changes, but otherwise, the car is as it was when I got it. I don't think I'll ever sell it, and even if I wanted to, I don't think Jen would ever let me.

I grew up in an era where everyone drove, and now we're seeing this transition to auto-driving cars. I can't imagine in ten years not driving a car, but I can see that my kids' kids might not know anything about driving, just like they don't know anything about a cassette player or a CD. My son, Vance, wants an old Bronco right now, and to know that he wants a vintage vehicle before he wants a new car, a modern car, is pretty cool—even though it is a Ford.

MATT FARAH

WRITER & PODCAST AND TV HOST

—||—

1988 LAMBORGHINI COUNTACH LP5000QV

My grandma says I could identify cars by their wheels when I was two years old. My dad used to let me drive on his lap when I was six, got me a go-kart when I was eight. When he gave me my first car magazine, it was a transformative moment.

I was a fat kid, never that great an athlete, but I was really good at racing go-karts. I thought, *I don't need to run fast if I can be in a fast thing and control it—that's how I'll go fast.* I used to run my go-kart until my parents begged me to stop.

Back when I was a kid in Atlanta, you never saw a Lamborghini on the street. Lamborghini made only two thousand Countachs over a period of sixteen years. They just weren't around. Today, if you live in Miami or LA or New York or San Francisco, you'll see modern Lamborghini Gallardos and Huracáns—they're still exotic, but anyone can lease them. That was before Lamborghinis were officially sold in the United States. There weren't factory Lamborghini dealers; it was a gray market of companies that would buy US-spec cars in Europe and ship them over.

As a kid who was really into cars, I had a huge poster of the white-on-white Countach on my wall—like this car, but white. The poster was as wide as my bed. The only Lamborghini I ever saw as a kid was in the showroom of a gray-market dealer called Formula One Imports, and I used to make my parents bring me there every week.

The dealer had the Countach, a Lamborghini LM02 SUV, some random Ferraris. At the time, you were either a Lamborghini Countach guy or you were a Ferrari Testarossa guy. But for me, the Countach was always the thing. It made the Ferraris look tame. You park that next to a sedan and it looks like it's from another planet. It wasn't built for anything besides going fast and looking crazy.

The car is even more outrageous today than when it was new. People lose their minds when they see it. It stops traffic in Los Angeles, where new Lamborghinis are common. This car makes people smile.

Finding a Countach is hard. I'm the third owner of this car. It's crazy to be able to say, "My Lamborghini Countach." Every day, I go into the garage to see it, and the fact that it's even there is special. It doesn't have a bad angle. It's fun and adventurous, and it doesn't bother me that I have to take off my shoes to drive it.

MARTIN LOGÉ

CAR RESTORER

———— ‖ ————

MASERATI 450S RE-CREATION

I've been playing with cars since I was five years old—building model race cars, subscribing to all the magazines. It's been a love affair my entire life. I love the whole experience: the beauty, the shapes, the sounds, the mechanics, the driving. Everything about a car. But I really gravitate to the aesthetics.

The Maserati 450S was a fast race car in the late fifties, the last iteration of a body style that started with the 200S. Throughout that decade, all the major players—Ferrari, Maserati, Aston Martin, and Jaguar—had these really beautiful aerodynamic cars that still look stunning today. They have a timeless clean design. Very sexy.

I had always wanted a vintage Italian race car. Ferraris were multiple millions of dollars, but a few companies in Europe were doing re-creations of priceless Italian race cars like the Ferrari 250 and 500 Testarossas. A friend of mine bought one of those, and it really fired me up for this project.

Maserati made only ten examples of the 450S. They're all still around, but they're staggeringly valuable. This car started life as a Maserati Mexico grand tourer, with a title and pink slip, VIN number AM112600, built in 1969. We shortened the frame to 2,400 millimeters, which was the standard for the FIA racing regulations of that period. We used the Maserati V8 engine out of the Quattroporte, which has a great crankshaft and reliable castings. We built that engine into about 425 horsepower, ported and polished, and everything from the pistons to the valves was redone.

We shaped the body, starting with the frame, which is basically a copy of what I could glean from the internet—there are a number of pictures of 450S frames being constructed, and I had two books on the car, so I had a good idea of what it was supposed to look like. The framework was then built to handle the body, which, because it's an aluminum *Superleggera*—that's Italian for Superlight—is just flat metal. The framework needed to clamp down and hold on to the body in the right position, so it was critical we get all those designs down.

This car was designed to be left-hand drive, even though Maserati never made a left-hand drive version. They made the original cars right-hand drive because they determined it was the correct position to run around a race circuit, but I live in California, and left-hand drive is the proper position to drive there. I'm not trying to fool anybody that this is the real deal. I made plenty of changes

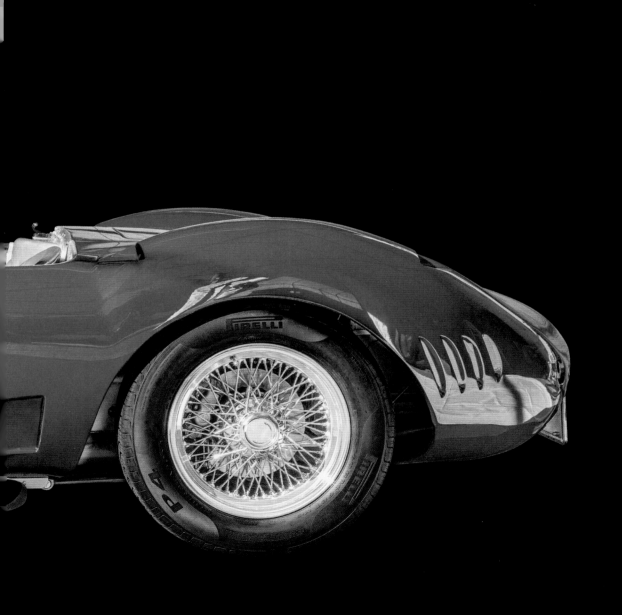

to the car to make it better. I used a Tronic transmission instead of the weak and vulnerable Colotti transaxle. The original cars had drum brakes, which were inefficient and constantly being taxed to the max, so I went with ventilated discs, and now the car stops unbelievably well.

It's actually quite comfortable to drive, but it beats you to death with the low windshield—it's loud and hot and noisy, and when you're done blasting through the countryside for a couple of hours, you're ready for a cocktail.

This was such a vast, winding project. I would say I probably put five to six thousand hours of time into this car—lunacy, really. But it was an endless source of pleasure, and it was nice to share it with the old-time craftsmen in Santa Barbara who helped build this car. At the end of the day, you have this piece you've created. You pull the cover off and people say, "My God, that's a beautiful car," and you realize, *Oh, right, I conceptualized and built this.* The passion and the love made it all worthwhile.

BRUCE PASK

MEN'S FASHION DIRECTOR,
BERGDORF GOODMAN

———— ‖ ————

1993 VOLVO 240 WAGON

When my parents were newly married, they bought a Volvo in Sweden and drove around Europe on their honeymoon. In those days, you could do that and then ship the car to the States, and it wasn't exorbitantly expensive. I didn't grow up riding in that car, but I always loved Volvos. I like that they have so much personality—they're completely eccentric, very intentionally shaped like a shoebox, but also there's the die-hard utilitarian aspect.

When I was in high school, I didn't have a cool car. Cars were just about, *Oh my gosh, we can drive to school!* There was no fetishizing of the automobile in my family at all. I didn't have a car in college. Then I moved to New York City. A car didn't feel like a necessity, but I was a freelance stylist and I thought, *When I get my first big job . . .*

I styled for Annie Leibovitz, and I did two big ad campaigns for *The Sopranos*. Those were my first really, really big gigs. I wanted to get something meaningful, symbolic of what I had achieved. I felt like I wanted a car.

I wound up purchasing this 1993 Volvo 240 Wagon at a Volvo dealership in New Jersey. I drove some of the newer ones on the lot, and I liked them, but when the salesman showed me this one, I just fell in love immediately. It was in pristine condition, with only one prior owner and maybe 89,000 miles on it. It has a camel leather interior. I'm a big fan of Scandinavian design, and it's obviously steeped in that Swedish Volvo aesthetic. Plus these cars are dependable and sturdy. Once, I got caught in an unexpected snowstorm upstate; other cars were spinning out, but the Volvo just plowed on through.

Having a car in the city provided me with a sense of freedom and self-determination. I started going up to Cape Cod a lot—I'd just jump in the car and drive there. It expanded my horizons, allowing me to not feel utterly dependent on a train schedule or an airplane reservation.

I do think it's funny that I have an old car, an old boat, and a really old house. I'm not averse to modern things—I just think my taste leans toward things that have stood the test of time. The Volvo is one of those things, with a timeless design and sensibility.

I got it in 2002 or 2003. It needs a lot of love and care, and I feel a duty to take care of it, though sometimes it's like, *Okay, not another thing!* But I can't ever see myself not having the car, even if it's on blocks sitting in the driveway, like a relic from my past. "Oh, he's still got that car; he never uses it, but he won't get rid of it." I really do love it.

MATT JACOBSON

HEAD OF MARKETING, FACEBOOK

———— II ————

**1955 PORSCHE 356
PRE-A COUPE**

It was through complete serendipity that the "straight outta Compton" 356 Porsche Pre-A came to be mine.

My close friend and partner in car projects for the last twenty years, Carlos Chavez, was in Compton picking up some miscellaneous car parts and saw the silver coupe, mostly disassembled, in a corner of the garage. He took a picture of it and its vehicle identification number, called me, and texted the photos.

I immediately called my friend Rod Emory and also sent him the photos. From the VIN, Rod was pretty sure it was a '55, making it a rare Pre-A example. It was the week before Thanksgiving and I was traveling, so I asked Rod if he could go look at the car and bring a trailer. If it was as it appeared, I wanted to buy it.

What Rod saw was an original car that had been lovingly disassembled forty years prior. Everything was with the car—but in boxes, bins, baby food jars. The car came with three motors: the original matching-numbers engine and two later 356 examples.

It was the platonic ideal of an original Pre-A Coupe, a rust-free California car that needed only some mechanical sorting out by Rod—brakes redone, fuel tank boiled out, fuel lines replaced, and a solid tune-up—to be roadworthy.

The Compton car has a cult following on Instagram and at the annual Luftgekühlt car show events, because it's just such a sweet, pristine example. It has a dash plaque from the 1978 Long Beach Grand Prix, a race Rod and I realized that we had both attended with our dads. This car has led to an even stronger friendship between me and Rod and his family than we had already.

A year to the day after seeing the '55 coupe, Rod got a call about another early 356. It was a one-family-owned '56 Speedster in the same original condition as the coupe, also matching numbers. It also hadn't been driven in nearly forty years. We got that car as well.

It's amazing to me that these gems are still out there, hiding in garages. It's also amazing the things you find on the Friday before Thanksgiving. Kismet.

SIMON DE BURTON

JOURNALIST & AUTHOR

———— ‖ ————

1964 LAND ROVER SERIES IIA SHORT WHEELBASE

My mother got me interested in cars. As a small child, I used to travel in the back of her Bentley R Type. My father had nice cars, but he wasn't particularly into them. But my mother had the Bentley, the S-Type Jaguar—several interesting Jags—a coachbuilt Austin Sheerline and a coachbuilt Armstrong Siddeley.

The reason I like Land Rovers is because of my oldest brother. He was twenty-four years older than me and quite unusual, quite eccentric. He didn't want to join the family business, a real estate auctioneering company that goes back to the early 1800s. He was a clever mathematician, quite handy. He could mend or make anything. At the age of sixteen or seventeen—bear in mind, this was in 1957, when there was fear of another world war—he was selected to study at a place called Fort Hall State, which was a Ministry of Defense establishment in East London. They were designing weapons, basically. My brother, not being an institutional person, was asked to leave after a year.

He set up a haulage business, and worked out a way of moving very large things using a weird roller system so you didn't have to lift them. He'd get them on the back of these long trailers, and he'd tow those trailers with Land Rovers. These were Series II Land Rovers, which are pretty uncomfortable—no heaters or anything of the kind. I remember going with him from the time I was five, six, seven years old. A Land Rover Series I or II smells totally different from other cars. Toyota Land Cruisers and Jeeps and the like, they didn't exist, particularly in England at the time. The Land Rover was *the* four-wheel-drive vehicle.

When I was twelve or thirteen years old, we happened upon a river—quite serious and good flow. My brother said, "Should we drive across it?" And we did, and it was amazing. We drove across, no snorkel, water coming up through the doors and everything.

My brother's business was a one-man band but quite busy. Once I was old enough to drive and attending college, I'd often help out. It was much more fun than going to class—and he'd pay me.

You have to be gentle with Land Rovers, especially Series IIs, which is the opposite of what you'd expect, because they're such rugged things. You've got the four-wheel-drive setup, which is all clunky and loose—you hear every bang and knock, the clanking of the universal joints, the knocking of the differentials. But if you're considerate toward them, they are rewarding things to drive.

"You have to be gentle with Land Rovers, especially Series IIs, which is the opposite of what you'd expect, because they're such rugged things."

—SIMON DE BURTON

ROBERT ROSS

AUTOMOTIVE CONSULTANT,
ROBB REPORT

————H————

1966 LAMBORGHINI 400 GT "INTERIM"

People connect with cars early in life. For me, it happened in 1966, when I was twelve years old. My dad was an architect; he was never paid much, but he was into cars, and I remember when he bought his first Porsche 911 from a place called FD Zipper in Beverly Hills. It was also a Lamborghini dealership, and they had the 400 GT out on a corner lot at Maple Drive and Wilshire Boulevard. I still have a photograph of me leaning against the fender of one of these old Lamborghinis. I just fell in love with them.

I bought this car back in 2001, after looking for many years. It was, until maybe the last ten years or so, one of the most undesirable early Italian exotics. Nobody wanted a goddamn Lamborghini 350 or 400 GT. The front headlights really soured the deal. My girlfriend at the time said, "I think it's such an adorable cross-eyed flounder." Well, that's what people thought of these cars. I was kind of an early adopter. They weren't really worth anything then.

The Lamborghini Miura was the car that set the company on its course. But prior to the Miura, Ferruccio Lamborghini wanted to make the best GT car in the world, to outdo Ferrari and Maserati. He did that with a car called the 350 GT, a front-engine V12 GT that looks essentially identical to my car. It was a remarkable thing, hugely advanced for its time.

That car came out in late '64 and put Lamborghini on the map. He zoomed up the displacement to 4 liters, at which point it was called the 400 GT. Then, to cater to market demand, he created a 2+2 version. There are about 150 two-seat versions, of which mine is one, most of which were 350s. There are a disputed number of cars called the "interims"—the factory says twenty-three; my research says eleven, of which mine is the first— that have Lamborghini transmissions and differentials, making them the first pure Lamborghinis. Prior to that, the company was using a Salisbury rear end from a Jaguar XKE and a ZF transmission. To me, the interim cars are the most interesting.

Through a shady broker, I found this car sitting in a barn in Escondido. I paid too much for it back then—I should have paid forty, fifty grand, and I think I ended up paying seventy thousand dollars. The guy took me to the cleaners.

At the time, a restoration cost more than the car was worth, but I said to myself, *I don't care. If I'm going to do it, I'm going to do it right.* I wanted

one reference example for the world. But I'm not a guy with money—I don't have all the resources—so this was going to be my one shot. Fortunately, my affiliation with *Robb Report* let me open some doors that would not have been opened otherwise, insofar as I was able, for a very brief period, to get into the factory and actually have access to the build sheet for the entire run of automobiles.

Over the last decade, these cars started to get on collectors' radars. *Wait a minute. It's a great car to drive—this car's better than a Ferrari of the era.* Everybody is talking about a Ferrari 330 GTC, but wait until you drive a Lamborghini 400 GT. It's better. It has a better engine, a better transmission; it handles better, looks more unusual. It fucking outclasses it.

THE BRIDGE

A couple of years ago, I attended a private car event called the Bridge, out on eastern Long Island. What stood out immediately was the pure celebration of the car—more as art than machine. The cars were thoughtfully displayed on the grounds of the Bridge golf course, a club built on the old Bridgehampton racetrack, which was rich in racing history, most famously with the thrilling Can-Am races of the seventies.

Founding member Jeffrey Einhorn describes the display as more of an exhibition than a concours, the latter being an event that judges cars by class and awards winners based on a complicated checklist of dos and don'ts. The Bridge is a celebration of cars—you really feel the love of the automobile when you're there.

On the Sunday after the show, they hold a coffee-and-cars event that's open to the public. The day I attended, there was an incredibly eclectic variety of cars—and an equally eclectic variety of owners! I set up in the morning with my 30-by-30-foot black backdrop and had a blast photographing some magical cars and talking with the people who love them.

1972 LAND ROVER SERIES III

MATT LEONARD
COFOUNDER AND PRESIDENT,
GAME 7 MARKETING AND
OLÉ CREATIVE

I distinctly remember the moment I fell in love with automobiles. I was six years old, and I discovered a Land Rover that was being used as a display car inside a Banana Republic at the Paramus Park mall. (I grew up in North Jersey. We love our malls.)

Back in the eighties, Banana Republic was a safari-inspired brand. Everything was cargo pants and light colors and safari jackets and animal prints. And the store used the Land Rover to help illustrate the theme—the front of the Land Rover would stick out of the front window like it had smashed through, and there was product in the back.

I remember turning a corner and seeing the car for the first time, and my jaw just dropped. At six years old, I had to know *everything* about it. I was confused, too—is it a Jeep? Is it a tractor? I couldn't wrap my head around it.

I was infatuated with that car and was always happy to see it. It's normally a chore for a kid, going to the mall with his mom, but I loved going for just that reason. I always told myself that when I was able to afford a Land Rover, I'd get one.

I started with the Defender 90, in my late twenties, and then worked my way backward to the Series III. You can find Land Rovers, and you can certainly find old Land Rovers, but this color—Marine Blue—is tough to find. It's also got the nonmatching wheels. It's very rugged, and it speaks to me. I don't ever want to lose it.

1964 CADILLAC DE VILLE CONVERTIBLE

KEITH NOSBISCH
SALVAGE BUSINESS
OWNER

My father and I went into the salvage business together when I was twenty years old, me in Florida, him in New York. I'm sixty-two now. We had a collection of cars in Florida. We bought a lot of old cars. We always liked old cars.

My father especially liked Cadillacs; we always had one when I was growing up. We picked up my baby brother from the hospital in a black '66 Cadillac Coupe de Ville. My older brother and I were in the backseat.

My father died last year. He had a 1960 Cadillac convertible that's now in my garage; I'm not going to sell it. I bought this one because I wanted to have something to remember him by.

1949 FORD F1

JOHN KASTANIS
HEALTH-CARE EXECUTIVE

I acquired this truck from a collector-car dealership in Pennsylvania because when I was a kid, a teenager barely driving—definitely without a driver's license—my uncle Pete had one in the sky-blue color.

At the time, the family was renovating a big old house in the Catskills—in the village of Cooks Falls, New York, overlooking the Beaverkill River—to use as a vacation home, and we used Uncle Pete's truck to run for groceries and supplies.

There was a natural state preserve at the edge of the village, and I used to pile all my young cousins in the back of the truck and go up a dirt trail for miles into the preserve. The truck would invariably stall out, and everybody had to get out and push. We usually would go after dinner, so it would be dark, and all the young cousins would always be afraid because I'd shut the headlights off and make them push, and once I got started, I'd leave them in the dust and pretend like I was abandoning them.

As I became an adult, I kept looking for this truck for years and years. I was very selective—I wanted one that was almost fully restored. I found this one in 2016. Two gentlemen had started the restoration, one in New Hampshire and the other in Pennsylvania. Coincidentally, when I found the truck at the dealership, the person who sold it to me had used it when he worked for another dealership that used it as a runner, a parts truck. So he knew the truck really well.

All of my cousins are still with us, and every time they see this thing, we remember our youth up in the Catskills. We had a lot of fun with that truck.

I think that's probably one of the strongest elements of an old car—how we related to it when we were younger, when we were kids and just wanted to get behind the wheel of what our dad or our uncle or our grandfather drove.

I'm definitely going to hold on to this. It's a keeper. And I know some people in our family who are interested in preserving the legacy.

1964 VOLKSWAGEN BEETLE DELUXE

DEREK VIBAL
CO-OWNER, DUPONT MOTORING

I've always been a gearhead, and VW is the one brand I've always had a love for. I grew up on Long Island, and my best friend's father owned a Volkswagen dealership. When my friend and I were about fifteen, we used to tinker with whatever VW sold at the time. We could go up to the dealership and grab factory tools and really work on the cars and learn about them, which was nice. This is going back a few years to when you needed microfiche to find parts, that sort of thing.

The Beetle is a basic car. It was really just meant to get you from point A to point B, but that's what drew me to it. The simplicity, without a doubt. Even though it was such a basic car, Volkswagen made it with such cool character and a simple design that worked for everyone.

I've been tinkering with this car since I got it. I restored the undercarriage so it wouldn't rot away. I corrected a bunch of little rust spots here and there. I actually lowered it. I drive it now and again. I'd like to drive it a little more, but life gets in the way.

I really appreciate cars. It's the only thing I've ever done in my whole life, working with cars one way or another. I have my own auto detailing and auto-collection-care firm that I run along with a couple of other guys, so I often get to drive some rare stuff—Ferraris, Aston Martins, Porsches. But when I hop into the Beetle, I always feel right at home.

1969 YENKO CHEVROLET CAMARO

MARK LIEB
FINANCIAL MANAGER

I've been around cars all my life. Oil is in my blood. I had a car detailing company when I was twelve years old. In high school, I used to spend seventh period in the machine shop, working on engines. I did a lot of drag racing when I was younger, at Connecticut Dragway—I ran a '62 Chevy Impala 409, then a '69 Plymouth Road Runner 440 Six Pack. I worked my way through business school at the University of Hartford buying, restoring, and flipping mid-year Corvettes.

It's always been American muscle for me. I grew up with it, and that's what I worked on. The Yenkos are very rare cars. This is one of the few left in the United States with the original drivetrain, and it's got a pile of paperwork from the original owner, a heart surgeon in Indianapolis who kept it in pristine condition.

I graduated from high school in 1968, and this car is a '69. I knew all about the Yenko Chevrolets when they came out—Don Yenko, a racer who owned the Yenko

Chevrolet dealership, upgraded a handful of stock Camaros with a Corvette V8 engine and beefier suspension—but I couldn't afford them because I was in college at the time. I've had a moderately successful business career that has since allowed me to build a muscle car collection. One day a guy named Steve brought this car to an auto show held at my winery on the North Fork of Long Island, and I went crazy for it. I chased him for eighteen months before he sold it to me. I've gone through the drivetrain and had the car repainted. It's got the original Yenko dealership invoices and everything. It's about as real as you get.

1953 MG TD

JIM SHELLY & BARRY RICE
ARCHITECT & CAR RESTORATION
SPECIALIST

JIM SHELLY: I've known Barry since he was riding around in the sidecar of his father's motorcycle with a football helmet on.

BARRY RICE: I've known Jim for probably twenty-five years or even longer. It's a small family.

JS: Car people are some of the friendliest groups of people. They're always willing to sit and talk to you about their cars. This car was a build by a group in New England who belong to the Vintage Sports Car Club of America. They nicknamed it the secret weapon, because they were hoping it was a Porsche 356 killer. It didn't work out so well for them.

It was never that fast. It's not a fast car, but it's an extremely fun car. It's one of those cars that people just grin at as you go by.

I bought it from a fellow named Ed Hyman for around two thousand dollars. I ran it until two years ago, when I bought an MGA, and then I said, "I have too many race cars." Barry was between cars, and I sent him off for the weekend in it. He came back ready to purchase.

BR: One of the appeals of buying cars, especially from people you know, is to be able to improve them. When you hand it on to somebody, you want them to do something active with it, or to improve it, because everybody's a temporary owner of these cars. The task with this one was to make it drivable—the pedals were too far away for me. But the car had been beautifully maintained mechanically; it just needed a little bit of tinkering.

JS: Barry took it from being a race car to a street car. Which is an entirely different purpose.

BR: I'm that crazy person who drives cars year-round out here in the Hamptons. My dentist couldn't believe it one day when I turned up in a Ferrari in a snowstorm because my other two cars weren't going that day.

My father collected cars. He had a 1927 Sunbeam, and my job was to get it ready for rallies. A year before I got my license at the age of fifteen in Australia, I got an MGA. I've nearly always had a car like that to drive around. Now that I have a house out on Long Island, I can actually keep one extra car in the garage. This is my one extra car.

JS: I really want to get it on the racetrack. The plan for next year is to have it ready for the track, at Lime Rock. I'm hopeful we'll do a full event with the VSCCA this year.

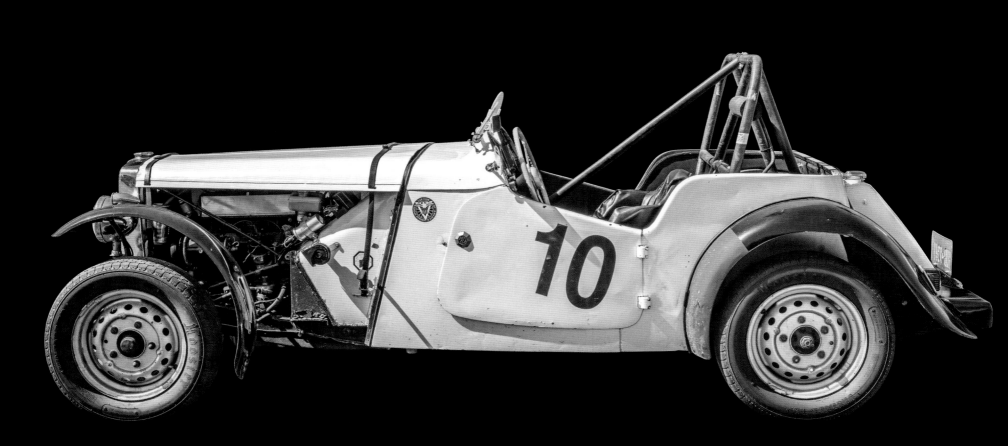

1951 CHRYSLER NEW YORKER

JAKE AUERBACH
GENERAL MANAGER, RALLY RD.

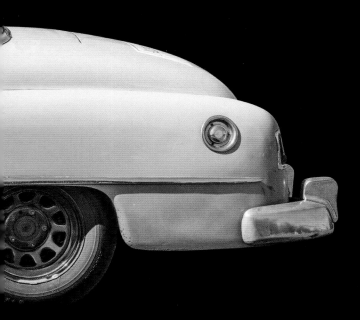

My memories of my dad are intertwined with memories of cars. They can't really be separated. I don't remember going to a Yankees game with him or anything else. Always just cars.

This 1951 Chrysler New Yorker has been in my family for a little over ten years now. My dad and I were looking for a car to take to long-distance touring and rally events together, and this is the one we found.

When I was twelve, thirteen years old, my dad sent me to work summers for his friend Jim Shelly, pumping gas in East Hampton, New York, getting to touch cars in the metal. The next year, I was vacuuming the shop. Then I was changing the oil. My interest in cars grew, but it was just a hobby. It was never meant to lead to a career. Ironically, it wasn't until after my dad passed that it occurred to me, *Wait, I actually know cars really well—more than most.*

Cars take up a lot of time, a lot of energy. You need to really want to do this. When my dad and I were a team, we would take turns starting the car in the morning, or one of us would say, "Let's go for a drive." When it's just you all of a sudden, it's a lot harder to play with cars. There are other, cheaper hobbies.

But I can't shake the car bug. I count myself very lucky that I get to work with cars. It's my calling in life—personally, professionally, whatever else. People sometimes ask, "Aren't you worried you're going to ruin your hobby?" But it's really all the same thing. Everything I do is inspired by the memories of growing up around cars, racing this thing, breaking that thing.

As a young man in the sixties, in the army and stationed in Texas, my dad owned some cars that would today be on the line at Pebble Beach, but back then they were just the used cars that guys would buy. He had a Porsche Speedster with Rudge wheels and a bee-stinger exhaust. Then he sold the Porsche, got a Gullwing. Sold the Gullwing, got a Ferrari 212 Vignale Spyder. These were all ten-year-old cars at the time.

My dad had enough sense to get out of cars when he was starting a family. He focused on his home, his company, his wife, and me and my two brothers. Then, when we were older and he had some free time, he started getting back into cars.

For some people, the collecting experience means Concours events, but for us it was about the rallies. We did 10,000 miles of competition. We did New York to Vancouver in this car. Pikes Peak, Chihuahua, Trans-America, Mount Equinox. It's got stickers on it that actually mean something. It's actually done this shit.

It's a very, very fast car. I love it because this is what an American sports car looked like in the early fifties. This is Mille Miglia eligible because that's what an American car that raced on Italian roadways looked like. That's a tuned-up sports car! They hadn't figured out aerodynamics quite yet, but they had figured out engines. As Enzo Ferrari famously said, "Aerodynamics are for people who don't know how to build engines."

BUCKMINSTER FULLER DYMAXION

This wild-looking vehicle was designed by Buckminster Fuller, who popularized the geodesic dome in the United States. The name stands for DYnamic MAXimum TensION, and the mid-engine car featured front-wheel drive but rear-wheel steering, plus a three-frame chassis and a Ford Flathead V8 engine with 85 horsepower. Of three examples produced, only one survives. This particular model is a reproduction of the original Buckminster Fuller design.

SPIKE FERESTEN

TV HOST & FORMER WRITER FOR *SEINFELD*
AND *LATE NIGHT WITH DAVID LETTERMAN*

———— ⊦⊦ ————

1958 PORSCHE SPEEDSTER

I've always loved sports cars, and I grew up in a town that didn't really have any. This was West Bridgewater, Massachusetts, a little blue-collar town, so American muscle cars were always around, but nothing exotic.

When I got to New York and saw the cars that David Letterman was collecting and was introduced to brands I'd never seen before—Ferraris, old Porsches—and Mr. Letterman said, "These are the cars that I think you're going to like more than what you're driving now," that was the moment when I said, *All right, let me try.*

It was at the airport in Santa Monica where I drove my first Porsche—a '64 356C. I got behind the wheel, hit the gas, and thought, *I can't believe it. This thing feels perfect. It feels like it was made for me.* Suddenly I had a carrot to chase, which was to try to duplicate every car that Mr. Letterman had. And I did it. I was able to buy and drive pretty much every car he had. And then I moved on to new things I hadn't discovered yet.

The first Porsche I owned was a '74 911 with a few hundred thousand miles on it and a lot of rust. I drove it in New York City. When the *Late Show* moved to CBS, part of the deal was that we could get really inexpensive parking spots at the

Sheraton Hotel across the street from the studio, which I immediately used as an excuse to buy that car. It was a rolling turd to everyone on the sidewalk, but I absolutely loved it. It had a five-speed transmission, and I drove it any chance I could in a city where you don't really need a car. I'd drive solo down the West Side Highway and right back. I loved that car.

The Speedster was a car introduced to me, again, by David Letterman. I took a closer look at it when I was writing for Jerry Seinfeld's show. Mr. Seinfeld had a couple of Speedsters. I believe they were '58, Meissen Blue, one with a red interior and one with a lighter, baseball-glove interior. Those cars stopped me dead in my tracks. When I got a chance to drive them, again I had this experience I frequently compare with putting on a pair of sneakers and thinking, *These feel right.* That car just felt right.

This car was for sale at Christmastime about twenty years ago, at a Butterfield & Butterfield auction that was mostly furniture. They had four cars. They advertised them in *duPont Registry*—at the time, I think it was just me and four other guys buying *duPont Registry*. I wanted this car to drive around Hollywood.

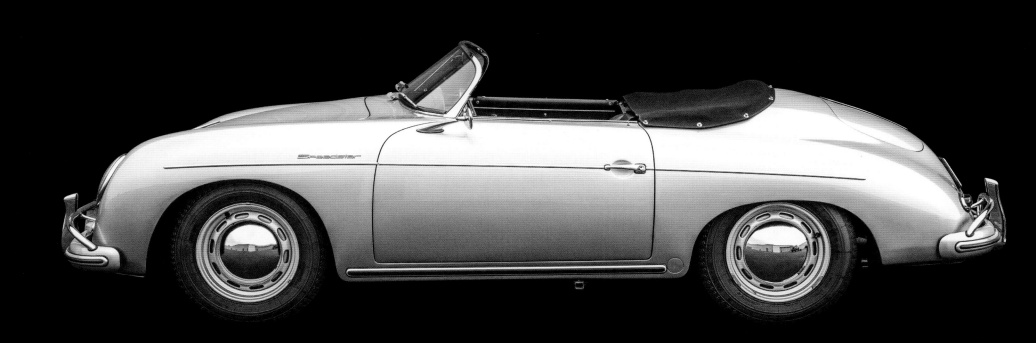

When the day of the auction came around, I got on the phone—the internet wasn't really up and running at that point—and *nobody* else was bidding on it. Everybody was there to buy the furniture. I remember that the original estimate was forty to sixty thousand, and we didn't get anywhere near that. And after the auction personnel drove it off the stage, they said, "We broke the transmission, so we'd like to credit you seventy-five hundred dollars." It turns out a little bit of linkage came unclipped. All we needed was a bolt, and for that little bolt we got seventy-five hundred bucks.

The brand resonates with me. It has nothing to do with the monetary value of the cars. It has to do with the aesthetic inside and out, and the focused driving experience. If these cars were worth a couple grand apiece, I'd still be driving them. If they were worth a hell of a lot more, I'd have to figure out a way to make enough money to get one.

This car has been with me the longest—about twenty years. It was there on my wedding day. And I still love to drive it. I don't keep these cars because I feel the need to keep them; I keep them because I still love to drive them. We all die; the cars outlive us. You don't want to be the fool on your deathbed thinking, *I'm a fucking idiot—who am I saving this for? The next guy?* Don't be the next guy. Drive your cars. Drive all of them.

BRADLEY PRICE

FOUNDER, AUTODROMO

———— ‖ ————

1976 FERRARI 208 GT4 & 1965 ALPINE A110

I've been a huge car nut my entire life. My grandmother used to say I was born with a car in my hand, because I was always holding a Matchbox toy car, even as a baby.

I grew up mainly around British cars: Austin-Healeys, Jaguars, Triumphs, MGs. Every so often, I would see an Italian car. The name *Ferrari* was very exotic to me. We didn't really know anyone who owned Alfas or Ferraris or Maseratis. These cars were more rare in the seventies and eighties. Today, with the internet, everyone can see what a GTO looks like. Back then, though, it was a super, super special thing to see a Testarossa or a GTO.

At one of my first jobs, my boss owned a 208 GT4; it's a Bertone design, so it doesn't look like a lot of other Ferraris. I always thought it was a really sharp design, really unusual. I wanted one in a dark color with the Dino badging and a European model with the small bumpers.

One day a black Dino GT4 showed up on Craigslist. It was a Dino-badged European model car. It was everything I was looking for, including the price. That's how I got hooked on it. It feels very special when you're driving one. The sound is great. It has a wonderful engine note. You feel transported back in time.

In high school, I started to really get into Alfas. The GTAs in particular and then the Alpine. I used to build model cars, and I had multiple models of the Alfa GTA and the Alpine A110. I would study the box art of the Alpine and think, *What a freaking cool-looking car this is*. I was just attracted to the design. I didn't know the rally history.

As an entrepreneur, I relate to the David-versus-Goliath story of Jean Rédélé and the Alpine company. He was so passionate about competing and building really cool road cars to fund his rally competition activities. He did it on a shoestring budget and a small scale, but he was able to compete against major manufacturers.

The Dino and the Alpine are like the difference between a gymnast and a weight lifter: they're both strong, but in very different ways. The Alpine is so precise—every little thing you do, there's immediate feedback. You can see why it won the World Rally Championship. The steering in the Dino is heavier; it's a much more physical car to drive.

I think I'm an old soul. I like the idea of what it might have been like to live in another time. Driving vintage cars is a great form of escapism from everyday responsibilities. It allows you into a more beautiful world, into a more special plane of being.

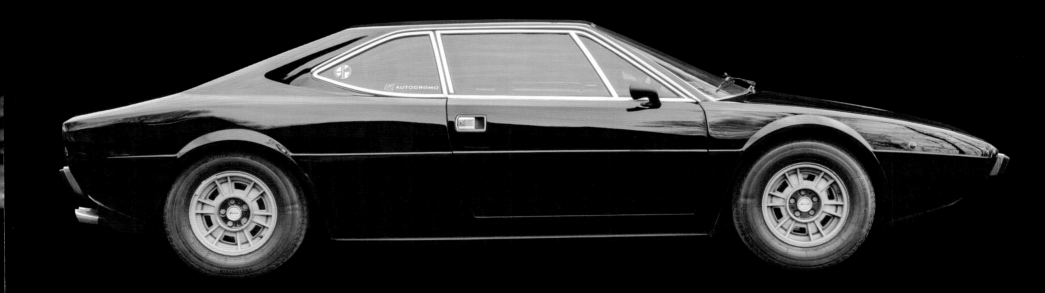

BEN CLYMER

FOUNDER, HODINKEE

————— || —————

1960 LANCIA FLAMINIA SPORT ZAGATO & 1960 ALFA ROMEO GIULIETTA SPRINT ZAGATO

Back in 1960, Lancia made the Flaminia in a few different ways. There was a Superleggera touring body that looked like a Maserati 3500, a Pininfarina four-door Berlinetta, and the Sport Zagato, which was made in Milan entirely of aluminum.

I was actually looking to purchase a Maserati 3500, but they were out of my budget. A friend said, "Hey, you should look at this Flaminia touring body; it's about half the price, but it's effectively the same car." I started asking around, and it turned out there was a Zagato-bodied Flaminia available in New York. I saw the car and completely fell in love with it. Also, it was a car that I really didn't know much about. I would say 99 percent of the "car guys" I know don't know what this car is—but when you find somebody who does, they freak out.

This was a real touring car, not a sports car. It was meant to go at high speeds for long distances, to basically bomb across the continent carrying its passengers in style and comfort. Lancia made the first six-cylinder engine, and they were one of the first car manufacturers to use disc brakes. They were producing the most high-end automobiles at the time. Lancia today is basically a budget European brand, but in 1960, this would have been one of the most expensive two-door touring cars in the world, as expensive as a Ferrari or a Rolls-Royce. The company was so obsessed with quality, they supposedly lost money on every car.

In the mid-sixties, the company was going out of business; 1967 or '68, Fiat acquired them. A pre–Fiat acquisition Lancia is a special thing in the car world, almost like having a Panerai from before Richemont owned them. It really helped me appreciate a coachbuilt car. They are so dramatically imperfect. One of the doors on my Lancia is more than an inch longer than the door on the other side. Lancias are just so different from everything else.

My prized possession, in terms of cars, is my 1960 Alfa Romeo Giulietta Sprint Zagato. Believe it or not, it was manufactured by Zagato two days after my Lancia Flaminia, in the same colors, at the same factory. Both cars were in the factory at the same time, which is wild.

The Lancia is a touring car, but the Sprint Zagato (SZ) was made to race. It is one of the original all-purpose sports cars, coming well before the Porsche 911. It was designed to race the Targa Florio as much as race on the track at Monza. And Alfa's 1300cc engines were dominant in the fifties and sixties. They were beating 1600cc Porsches in almost every race, to the point where Porsche said, "Hey, we need to do something about this." That's when they started making four-cam engines to compete with the Alfa Romeos.

I wanted to find an original SZ. I found this one through the Gooding & Company auction house. One of the guys said, "Hey, I know of a totally unrestored Alfa Romeo Sprint Zagato, and I think it has race history." I lost my mind, was totally over the moon. This car ran Targa Florio three times, in '61, '62, and '63. It ran other races around Italy and was then shipped to New York. From about 1968 to 2014, the car did not move. It just sat on blocks.

The car looks like a big piece of junk, but it is the most amazing car you can imagine. It's really a baby Ferrari, so aggressive and tuned like you wouldn't believe. I have friends with far more valuable cars who say the driving experience in this is about as pure as anything can possibly be. It looks like an angry little jelly bean, but it's a tiny rocket.

The original owner was Gianni Bulgari, of the Bulgari family of jewelers. I'm in the watch and jewelry world, and I asked the Bulgari company if they could put me in touch with Gianni. We exchange emails about this car all the time now. Gianni sent me about eighty old photographs of the car when it was new, running the Targa Florio, stuff like that.

Gianni Bulgari was a gentleman racer, working at the family business and racing in his free time. I always liked the idea of the gentleman racer, doctors and bankers and industrialist heirs who had somewhat normal lives during the week but would go out on the weekends and really *race*. In many ways, I fancy myself a modern gentleman driver, a gentleman racer. During the week, I'm at the office, holding meetings about inventory levels, but when the weekend comes, I go upstate and fire up the Alfa Romeo or the Lancia, and I get to be someone else for a bit.

But owning one of these kinds of cars is not for the faint of heart. It's loud; it's hot; it smells like gasoline. Sometimes it won't start. Sometimes the car catches on fire, which has happened to me. But you want to have something that has a story behind it. I wanted cars that bring out really intense emotions, both in myself and in other people—cars that allow me to escape the mundane world, if just for a little while.

"It looks like an angry little jelly bean, but it's a tiny rocket."

—BEN CLYMER

ALFA ROMEO/FIAT ARCHIVE

I was in school in Europe for a time in the eighties, and the cars I saw on the street during my trips to Italy—especially the Fiat Pandas, Cinquecentos, and Spiders—defined the Italian experience for me, because Fiat represented how people actually got around in Italy. Like Ford in America, Fiat created a democracy of automobile ownership.

I was lucky to get into the Fiat Heritage Hub, a unique exhibition space that is not yet open to the public. Located in a huge industrial warehouse in Turin, it looks like three football fields just full of cars. They have the personal car owned by Gianni Agnelli, the playboy industrialist and longtime chief executive of Fiat; they have race cars and rally cars and prototypes and even Fiats added to the archive straight off the assembly line.

The Alfa Romeo Museum, outside Milan, is equally impressive. It is beautifully designed and curated, presenting a timeline of the brand from a historical point of view. To see all those cars under one roof was incredibly inspiring.

I've grouped these two collections together because Alfa Romeo and its archive have been acquired by Fiat and its holding company. And these two car companies have shaped the auto industry in Europe in terms of their manufacturing and design. In both cases, choosing what to include in the book came from a very personal place. The cars I selected are not necessarily the most race-winning or famous but are models that I was drawn to in my youth, or that tell a particularly interesting story.

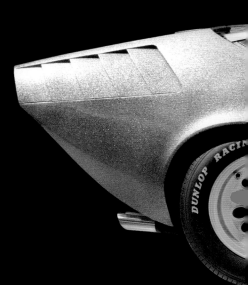

1952 ALFA ROMEO 1900 C52 "DISCO VOLANTE"

A racing prototype with mechanicals derived from the model 1900, this is the first mass-produced post–World War II Alfa sport sedan with a monocoque body. The unique body of the Disco Volante, or "flying saucer," was crafted by Carrozzeria Touring.

1969 ALFA ROMEO IGUANA

The Iguana is a prototype designed by legendary car designer Giorgetto Giugiaro of Italdesign on the Alfa Romeo Tipo 33 chassis for the 1969 Turin Motor Show. Alfa Romeo then acquired the Iguana. Giugiaro is also the designer of the iconic DeLorean DMC-12, and some of the Iguana's designs were inspiration for the DeLorean, as well as the Panda and the original VW Golf.

1975 ALFA ROMEO 33 TT 12

This race car debuted during the 1974 season at the
Monza 1000 and went on to win the Manufacturers'
Championship at the 1975 World Rally Championship,
with Mario Andretti among its drivers.

1982 FIAT 131 S 2000 TC AUTOMATIC

The 131 was Fiat's "family sedan," produced from the
mid-seventies through the early eighties. The S 2000
was the most high-end model. This was the personal
car of Gianni Agnelli, the chairman of Fiat. It was
equipped with automatic transmission because Agnelli
couldn't operate the clutch due to a leg injury.

1952 FIAT 600 PROTOTYPE

The Fiat 600 was meant to be the car that the typical Italian family used for transportation. This is the prototype, and the engine was placed in the rear. The aesthetic changed slightly for the mass-produced version, the Fiat 500, but proportions and basic lines remained the same.

1958 ABARTH-DESIGNED FIAT 500

The Fiat 500 was one of the first practical, reasonably priced cars, and perfect for city driving because of its small size (just 10 feet long and about 1,000 pounds). Legendary car manufacturer Carlo Abarth took the original Fiat 500 and "tuned" it, giving it more power and better handling. The Fiat 500 Abarth was a recorded winner in Monza.

1976 FIAT NUOVA CAMPAGNOLA

"Campagnola" is synonymous with Fiat off-road. The first version was built in the 1950s; this second version was mainly used by the Italian army.

TED GUSHUE

PHOTOGRAPHER

——H——

1976 PORSCHE 911S

My father and I are the second owners of this car. He bought it in 1992 from a dear friend who's no longer with us. It's a lot like the car I grew up with. My parents brought me home from the hospital in a 1982 911SC in Guards Red. When that car was sold, this car was purchased, so it was a seamless transition. It's like it's been a member of my family for as long as I can remember.

This car originally came with a 2.7-liter engine, which my dad and I swapped out in 2014 for a 3.2-liter, so it's hopped up. It was restored by the German company Ruf, which has some of the best Porsche engineers and technicians in the world. The car has traveled the world with me.

My mother's grandfather was a GM executive in the thirties, and my dad's dad was a mechanical engineer. Cars were a huge part of my dad's life. Back in the seventies, it wasn't a big deal to wrench on your cars because everyone had the technological know-how. You'd go to someone's house and they'd have project cars sitting around. My dad has endless photos of Porsches, Lotuses, Ferraris—the coolest stuff you can imagine.

It wasn't a high-net-worth activity. In 1978, a '72 long-hood Porsche 911 was not an expensive car. My dad and his friends would go buy cars that had recently crashed or been written off, and then fix them up at home. It was more of a blue-collar thing; they just happened to dig European sports cars. They basically ran a little body shop out of my grandparents' garage.

Cars became a big part of my life because of my dad. When I was born, my parents were still going to Lime Rock Park for vintage racing on the weekends with all their friends. I didn't think about it at all until I was in high school and realized that I was the only kid who knew anything about Porsches. In the same way that someone who was raised in a French household speaks French, if you're raised around cars, you speak Car.

A car like this is much closer to tailoring than utility. If you've made the decision to have a vintage Porsche, to maintain it and treat it properly, it's no different from going to Henry Poole & Co. on Savile Row and having a suit made; you're telling people you take your mode of transportation seriously.

Having this car signals to my community that I'm a part of it, but it also smells like my home, like my dad—like my childhood. I see my parents only maybe four times a year, so the car is like mobile family. But it's more than just nostalgia—it's such a great thing to drive. I just love driving it.

AL UZIELLI

OWNER, LA DOLCE VITA, LOS ANGELES

——— ǁ ———

2005 FORD GT

When Ford announced the GT for 2005, I wasn't sure I wanted it. I'd never owned such a valuable car, and I had just come off a two-year build of a 1966 Mustang convertible. I had wanted a very drivable, comfortable, classic vehicle built to contemporary standards, but the Mustang ended up being much more of a race car. It was a beast, with a 289 drop engine, NASCAR suspension, racing shifters. My daughter Olivia had just been born, and her sister Eleanor was two years old, and whenever I'd start that car up, they would cry, it was so loud. Fifty percent of the time when I took it out, something would not quite click. My wife, Kimm, wasn't happy with it. Ultimately, it wasn't what I had expected. It didn't serve a purpose.

The more I read about the GT, the more I thought the negotiation could be, *Okay, I'll sell the Mustang and get the incredibly comfortable and drivable GT.* So I placed my name on the list and put the Mustang up for sale.

There was no guarantee I'd get a GT, though perhaps there was some preferential treatment— my mother is a daughter of Henry Ford II. The GT is a 2005 vehicle, but it's built pretty much to the specs of what the GT40 was in 1966. That year holds a lot of mystique for me. It's the year I was born, for one thing. It's also the year Ford beat the Italians at Le Mans in the GT40. And it's the year La Dolce Vita, the restaurant I now own, opened.

I've had the GT for thirteen years now. The lines are incredibly classic. Los Angeles has an amazing wealth of beautiful automobiles from all over the world, but when you drive down Sunset Boulevard in this race car with *Ford* emblazoned on the side, people literally stop in their tracks and lean out their windows to take pictures.

Ford released another GT model in 2016, a street version of what we're racing at Le Mans today. It's a beautiful automobile, a lot more expensive, with a lot more technology. But I wouldn't trade mine for the world—everything about it, including how drivable it is, is just perfect for me. The way it blends the past and present, 1966 lines on a 2005 car, makes it so relevant and poignant. In a lot of ways, it's what I strive for at La Dolce Vita: you have this old structure, all this history, but you have to make it relevant to keep your customers coming back.

This is the first car I've owned that I take out just to drive, not to get somewhere. With the craziness of work, family, and business, there are so few opportunities to commune with yourself. I use this car like therapy. We all want to meditate, to

be in the moment and relax. I drive it when I need to escape, and I'm never more in the moment than when I'm in that car. You're low to the ground; the steering wheel is perfectly placed.

There are some great drives around LA. Take the 101 to Kanan Dume Road, along Mulholland Highway to Decker Canyon, and you get all these different types of roads, from straightaways to winding turns, leading you down to the Pacific Coast Highway and then back to LA. You drive through a handful of tunnels as you go through. You roll down the windows and hear the sound of the vehicle, and it's amazing, like a symphony of trumpets. Then you break through and you're looking at the Pacific Ocean. Go on a Sunday morning, around seven, and there are just a handful of people doing exactly what you're doing.

I would never drive another brand of car. Obviously, when Ford owned all the European brands, it was nice to be able to drive a Jag and a Range Rover and all that, but I will always remain loyal to and supportive of the Ford business and whatever that includes.

FRANÇOIS POURCHER

FOUNDER, TEYRAS

—ıı—

1950 JAGUAR XK120 OTS

My passion for cars comes from two men dear to me: my great-grandfather Papa Guy, who was the first to own and drive Voisin brand cars—still exceptional today!—and my father, Michel, who loves beautiful lines and cars.

My love for this car starts with the love of Jaguar—its spirit, elegance, and sportiness—and the appreciation of the brand that my father instilled in me early on. He bought a Jaguar in 1977 and still rolls in it today.

I fell in love with the XK120 when I saw vintage photos of it racing at the 24 Hours of Le Mans. The shape of the car is pure and streamlined, and the XK engine is one of the most durable and sporty ever built.

The XK120 went from a prototype to becoming the fastest car in the world in 1948, taking part in all the legendary races across the world, like the Mille Miglia, the 24 Hours of Le Mans, Goodwood, Sebring. And the car has been very popular with celebrities, like Clark Gable, Marilyn Monroe, Françoise Sagan, and Ralph Lauren.

This car is like a friend to me. I even gave her a name: Paulette. She has made it around almost all of Europe. I drive a lot, twenty-five to thirty thousand kilometers a year. I participate in many races, like the Tour Auto, Modena Cento Ore, and, soon, the Le Mans Classic and Mille Miglia—always with my friend Simon Le Bon of Duran Duran.

I relish the strong emotion in driving, the feeling of freedom. Sometimes it's like having a glass of good Margaux. It relaxes you. Experiencing the mechanics. Meeting people. Discovering roads and incredible places. Listening to the engine sing.

GUILLAUME POURCHER

SURGEON

———— H ————

1962 JAGUAR E-TYPE

I had the chance to fall in love with cars from a very young age. Since the advent of the automobile, my family has been passionate about the quest for performance and progress. My great-grandfather Guy Chaslus had many notable cars, including the C23 Voisin—the designer, Gabriel Voisin, was a French aviation pioneer who converted to the automotive revolution after World War I. And my father introduced me to the world of Jaguar with his XJ6 Series II, which we used for family travels.

To now have this E-Type is a childhood dream come true. The coupe's incredible design—the work of Malcolm Sayer and Sir William Lyons—is very special to me because the shape is like the front of a plane, a blend of car and spaceship. The E-Type ushered in the era of the modern sports car. This is one of the first models to have an aluminum dashboard and center console and bucket seats. There are design elements—like the "aviation" dashboard switches and the recessed glass headlights—and accessories and flourishes that are like car jewelry.

I bought my E-Type in September 2009 randomly, during a medical convention in San Francisco.

It was love at first sight. The car was first delivered in January 1962, in New York. I am the third owner.

Originally the color of this E-Type Series I was Golden Sand, but the second owner, who bought it in 1964, wanted to paint the car an "old gold" color like on the cylinder head cover. That color is characteristic of the XK engine available in the E-Type until 1964. This is the first model with that famous 3.8-liter six-cylinder XK engine, engine number J63887746. Three dual-overhead cam SU carburetors and 265 horsepower, like in the Jaguar XK150.

The second owner also modernized it by replacing the Moss gearbox with the Jaguar gearbox, which makes it much more fluid and efficient.

As a surgeon, I need to provide compassion, excellence, communication, and truth, and I connect to all of these values at the wheel. Driving an E-Type requires all the senses—touch, smell, vision, hearing, and, because of the escapement of oil into the confined space, even taste. Driving this car physically connects me to the world, to truth and freedom.

I am fortunate to have four children who live this same passion, as well as my brother, François, and we ride together whenever possible.

MICHAEL RANDALLS

ARTIST

——— ‖ ———

1978 MG MIDGET "ART CAR"

I've done about eight art cars. This one was special for me because it was the first car I drove and because of the connection to my dad. I was eleven years old when my father used me as his designated driver—at that age, it was like a full-size car!

For almost twenty years, I drove around the country painting signs. I lived in my van, which was painted up with signs on the side. It's not a glamorous life, but I created signs in forty-eight states—got to see the entire Continental US and splash paint all over the country.

Sign painting is commercial. There's not much room for personal expression. Painting my cars allowed me to express myself. I use my sign paint on the cars. I like British cars. I did a Jag, too, and I always had Volkswagens. My dad would rag on me because he didn't think Volkswagens were cool like the MG, so when I got the MG, I painted a Volkswagen emblem on it. This car has the great wave on one side, then it flows the opposite way on the other side. It's movement, color, speed, sport. The ebb and flow of life. Life as art.

I owned the MG for a few years, then wound up selling it to a guy from New Jersey named Mark—same as my dad's name. He continued my design into the interior of the car. He even painted the valve cover in the same style, which is pretty cool. He loves the car, and his daughter loves it. It's become central to his life, which is what I wanted it to do.

To see art that hangs on someone's wall where only one person gets to enjoy it, or only those in close proximity get to see it, there's some frustration. It's like a selfish thing. I figured, as an artist, paint the car and then it's out there—it's in your face; there's no holding it back. It's everywhere.

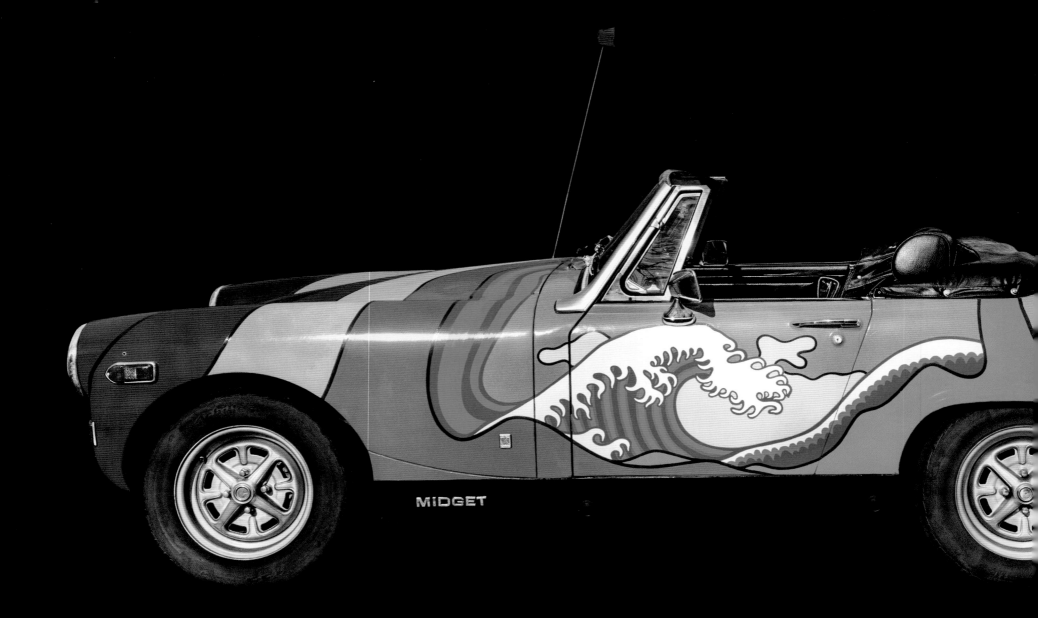

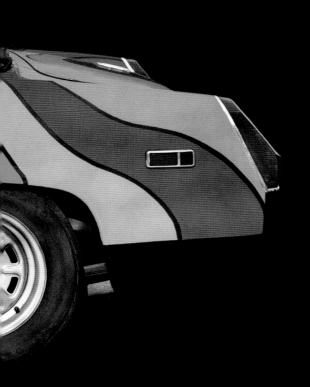

"This car has the great wave on one side, then it flows the opposite way on the other side. It's movement, color, speed, sport. The ebb and flow of life. Life as art."

—MICHAEL RANDALLS

SHAQUILLE O'NEAL

NBA HALL OF FAMER & ENTREPRENEUR

———— ɦ ————

INTERNATIONAL CV SERIES 6.6

I'm sometimes known as Diesel, and I'm big on wow factor when choosing my vehicles. When I was younger, I was really into the newest sports cars, but now my favorite types of cars are trucks. They are reliable, they are BIG, and they get me from point A to point B.

When I saw the International, a dually pickup with a powerful diesel engine, it immediately resonated with me. I couldn't resist; I had to have it! I sent it to my guys to put extra-special touches on it. Look out for that big gray beast rolling down a road near you.

My first car was a Ford Bronco II. Years later, when I got my first big paycheck, I immediately went to a dealership and bought a black Mercedes. Always wanted one. When I pulled into the driveway, my dad came out and said, "Where is mine?" So I went back to the same dealership with my dad and bought another one just like it. When we showed up back at the house, my mom came out and said, "Those are nice; what about mine?" So I took my third trip to the dealership.

I love driving. There's something therapeutic about it. Whether it's just me, cruising around with music playing and the windows down, or me and my family and friends packed into the Sprinter, there's a level of comfort inside that is hard to find anywhere else.

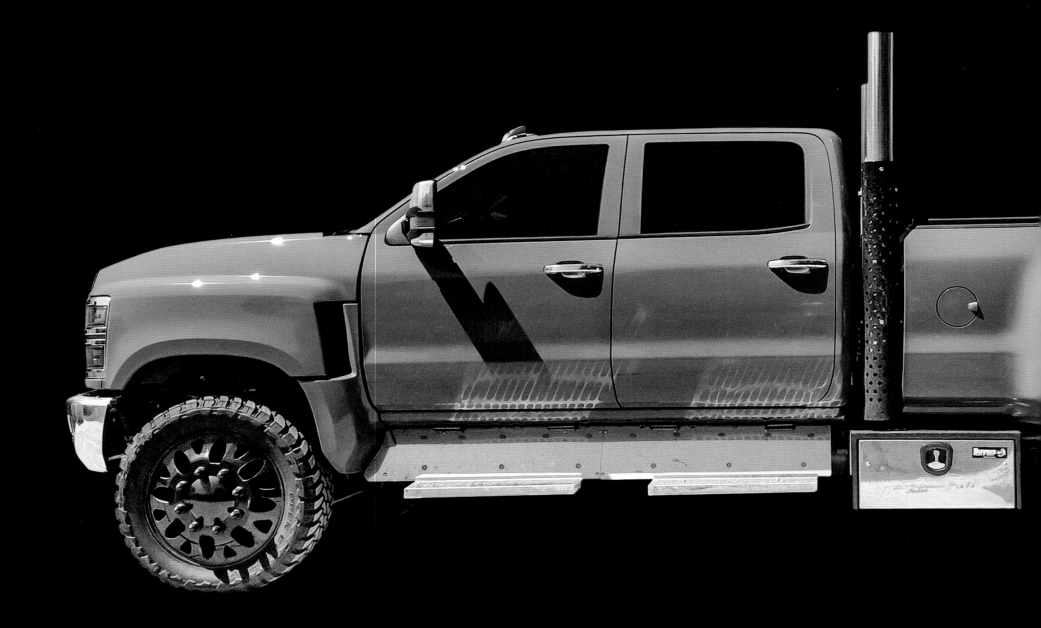

"I'm sometimes known as Diesel, and I'm big on wow factor when choosing my vehicles."

—SHAQUILLE O'NEAL

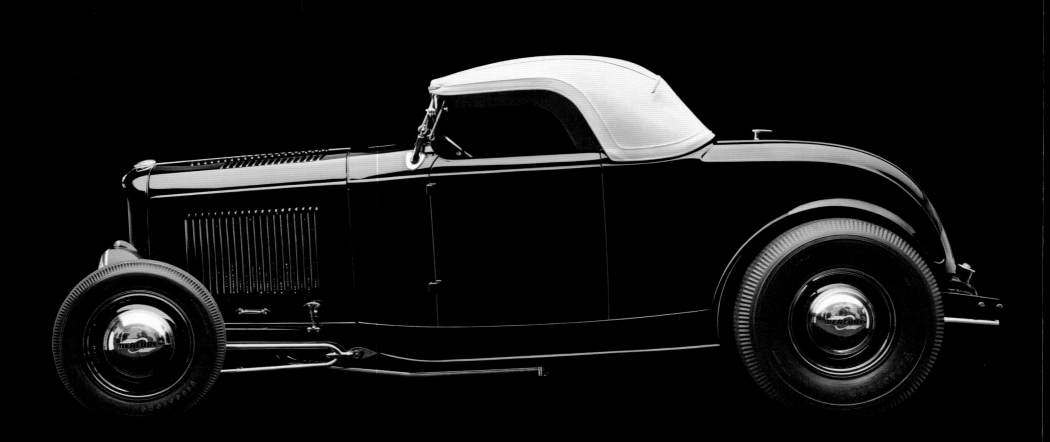

KEN GROSS

AUTHOR & AUTOMOTIVE CURATOR

———— ɪɪ ————

1932 FORD
DELUXE ROADSTER

I started getting interested in hot rods and sports cars in 1954. I bought my first issue of *Road & Track* in May 1954 and my first issue of *Hot Rod* in December of that year—I still have that issue, and every subsequent issue.

When I was a kid, the car to have was the 1932 Ford Roadster. I always wanted one, and when I was in high school, I made a list of the modifications I would make if I was ever lucky enough to buy one. It wasn't until I was in my fifties that I was able to make it happen. I bought this car in 1994, and I pretty much stuck with the same plan I had outlined as a teenager.

When I was writing a book called *Art of the Hot Rod*, I went to twenty different hot rod shops around the country. I was visiting them to do research for the book, but at the same time I was also interviewing them to build my car. The person I eventually chose for the job was Dave Simard of Leominster, Massachusetts. He and I agreed philosophically on everything I wanted, which was to build the best car that could have been built around 1948, 1949, using only original, authentic parts.

When I bought this car, it was a rolling chassis with the original steel body. Someone had put a Corvette engine in it, so the first thing I did was take that out. I had a Ford flathead built by Mark Kirby from Motor City Flathead, in Detroit, one of the best guys in the country for them. A stock flathead would have been 239 cubic inches; he built a bored and stroked engine with 304 cubic inches. As flatheads go, it's a big motor.

It took several years to collect everything I wanted for the car. I was able to find a supercharger from SCoT, the Supercharger Company of Turin, Italy. This was a rare accessory and would have been very expensive in 1946, '47, '48, nearly five hundred dollars, but I wanted one. I also wanted Kinmont brakes. They were an early disc brake that looked more like a clutch and pressure plate than a brake caliper. Some really terrific feature cars from the early *Hot Rod* magazines used them, but only about two hundred sets of those were ever made, so I had to hunt for several years before I found a pair.

Everything on the car represents the height of what was possible at the time. It has Eddie Meyer high-compression aluminum heads, made in Hollywood, and a 1934 Auburn instrument panel with the original instruments restored. It took me a long time to find that—I had to get an acquaintance in Dayton, Ohio, to secure it from a classified ad and mail it to me—and another year to have it restored, but all the best hot rods had one. I'd basically been building the car in my mind for my entire adulthood, and then Dave Simard and I got to build it in real life. A lot of effort has gone into every square inch of this car.

In 2007, for the seventy-fifth anniversary of the '32 Ford, a group of panelists voted the seventy-five best '32 Fords of all time, and out of four hundred cars, my car made the list. (I was one of the panelists, but there were around fifty of us, so I don't think my vote threw anything off.) I love when people come up to me at auto events and say, "I love your car," or that they've seen it in magazines. A little movie my wife made of me driving it got more than two thousand likes on Instagram, which I thought was extraordinary.

But mostly, I like driving it. This car has six thousand miles on it, which is quite a bit of driving for a fenderless '32 Ford with no windows, but I still love it. It fires right up. It's fast and very enjoyable.

I feel fortunate to have a passion that's also my business. It's fascinated me for most of my life, back to when I was a kid. It reminds me of Dicky Cline, who saw me sketching cars when I was sixteen years old and asked if I was drawing a '32 Ford. I said yes, and he asked me why. When I told him that I'd really like to have one someday, he looked at me and said, "You'll never have a '32 Ford." To this day, I laugh sometimes and think, *I don't know where you are, Dicky Cline, but I'm in my '32 Ford.*

ACKNOWLEDGMENTS

I would like to thank my dad, who shared his passion for cars with me from the moment I could utter the word "truck"; my mom, who dug through my high school archives in my childhood home to find the photos of me and my first car; and my daughter, Clara, who tolerated my absence as I traveled around the globe photographing cars; as well as Nick Adler, Stefano Agazzi, Ken Bailey, Mary Randolph Carter, Kate Cunningham, Mark Dalzell, Jeffrey Einhorn of the Bridge, Marco Fazio, Roberto Giolito of FCA Heritage, Eric Hadley, Jasper Hadley, the organizers of the Hilton Head Concours d'Elegance, Nicholas Kalikow, Ken Kobayashi, Stephanie Koven, Stephen Lewis, Jeremy Malcolm, Spence Medford and his team at the Henry Ford Museum, Bruce Meyer, Willem Mitchell, Dewey and Stephanie Nicks, the Petersen Automotive Museum; Steve Reich, Dennis Roach, Lenny Shiller, Al Uzielli, and John Weiss. Thanks to Josh Condon, fellow car lover, who helped me shape the words in this book and supported me along the way. And to my excellent postproduction team at Spruce. To Leica and Hasselblad for providing me with the tools to capture these cars in this book. Finally, I have a ton of gratitude for my epic team at Artisan: my always thoughtful, fun-filled, and enthusiastic publisher, Lia Ronnen; my encouraging and patient editor, Shoshana Gutmajer; Nina Simoneaux; Suet Chong; Elise Ramsbottom; Sibylle Kazeroid; Theresa Collier; Allison McGeehon; and Nancy Murray.

INDEX

MATT HRANEK is the author of *A Man & His Watch*, as well as a photographer, a director, and the founder/editor of the men's lifestyle magazine *Wm Brown*. He and his family divide their time between Brooklyn and the Wm Brown farm in upstate New York, though he can also be spotted quite often in old-school bars around Europe, Negroni in hand. Find him on Instagram at @wmbrownproject.